The Chocolate Truth

an anthology of perspectives from community college CEOs

The Chocolate Truth

an anthology of perspectives from community college CEOs

Contributing Writers

Helen Benjamin
Douglas Chambers
Lawrence Cox
Ned Doffoney
Charlene Dukes
Marie Foster Gnage
Erma Johnson Hadley
Andrew Jones
Jowel Laguerre
Wright L Lassiter, Jr.
Audre Levy
Gordon May
DeRionne P. Pollard
Thelma Scott-Skillman
Joe Seabrooks
Ernest L. Thomas
Debraha Watson
Jennifer Wimbush

Presented by the Presidents' Round Table
A Collaboration of African American Community College

Chief Executive Officers
Project Editor: Joe Seabrooks, Ph.D.
Project Co-Editors: Helen Benjamin, Ph.D. and DeRionne P. Pollard, Ph.D.

MY VISION WORKS PUBLISHING
Farmington Hills, Mi

The Presidents' Round Table

Contributors:
The Presidents' Round Table
Project Editor: Joe Seabrooks
Project Co-Editors: Helen Benjamin and DeRionne P. Pollard

My Vision Works Publishing
Book Interior and Cover Design-My Vision Works Publishing
Editor-in-Chief-Rhonda Boggess
Senior Editors: Eddie Allen and Nora Feldhusen
Publishing Assistant-Jana`White

Printed in the United States of America.

ISBN-13: 978-1470012526
ISBN-10: 1470012529

Library of Congress Cataloging-in-Publication Data

The Presidents' Round Table

For additional information contact us at:
http://apps.ccc.edu/roundtable/

The Chocolate Truth: an anthology of perspectives from community college CEOs
1.   African American 2.   Non-fiction   3.   Anthology   4.   Higher Learning

Contents

Foreword

There is much truth to the adage that time passes when you're having a good time because it doesn't seem like it has been almost 40 years since I began my professional career in higher education. Twelve years into my profession, I secured my first position as a campus CEO and was immediately introduced to the members of the Presidents' Round Table (PRT) of the National Council of Black American Affairs (NCBAA), an affiliate of the American Association of Community Colleges (AACC). Though I had been a leader most of my life through such activities as Girl Scouts, church, and other organizations, I felt as though I had truly arrived when I was named Provost/CEO of a community college in Virginia.

One of the major resources available to me was the official *Directory* of the PRT. It placed at my fingertips the names, phone numbers and e-mail addresses of a group of community college leaders who were not only experiencing the same things I was but who also looked like me—that is, people of color. While this might not seem like a big deal, it is important to remember that as human beings, we tend to look to affiliate with those with whom we have something in common. Though there were other campus CEOs with whom I could commiserate about activities, processes, and policies at the college, I was not able to share my innermost thoughts and feelings. For example, when I walked into a room people saw me as female and African American, NOT as the CEO because I was the only one like me. The PRT members were there for me.

This book consists of articles by some of those colleagues, both men and women of African American descent who shed insights on their experiences in hopes of being of assistance to those who might aspire to follow in their footsteps. They include lessons in handling strategic planning processes and budgets, boards, irate faculty and staff, and knowing when it's time to leave the position and move on to something else; however, they also discuss personal issues, such as time management and how to survive socially in communities where there are few people who share their background and experiences.

There are approximately 1,200 community colleges in this country but only about 100 African American CEOs, hence, the belief that we needed to tell our own story. It is my hope that when you finish reading these stories, you will have learned how to survive both professionally AND personally in one of the most rewarding but demanding career opportunities in higher education.

A favorite possession of mine is a framed quotation that was given to me by a former employee that says, "Being in charge isn't all glory." I think you'll find that this book defines some of those glory moments while offering advice on how to ensure more of them.

Best wishes for a successful journey toward the presidency.

Belle S. Wheelan, Ph.D.
President, Commission on Colleges
Southern Association of Colleges and Schools

Acknowledgments

Ideas are easy to come by. Making an idea a reality is a different matter, especially with the publication of the anthology you are about to read. Undertaking the publishing of an anthology by an organization such as the Presidents' Round Table (PRT) requires strong leadership and the participation of many individuals.

The idea for *The Chocolate Truth* surfaced in our annual meeting in Chicago in 2009. Always concerned about the success of current members and those who aspire to CEO positions in community colleges, members in attendance at the meeting brainstormed ways in which the PRT could be of more assistance. The idea of a monograph on issues related to the challenges and opportunities of being an African American and a community college CEO emerged. The PRT convener assigned Joe Seabrooks and DeRionne Pollard the awesome task of making the idea a reality. At the time they held the distinction of being the newest as well as the youngest members of the PRT. Products of the "hip-hop" era and a strong "old school" influence, they returned to the January 2010 special meeting in Dallas with a fully formed book, replete with cover designs, recommended titles for the book, and chapter headings. We were on our way!

Sincere thanks is extended to Joe Seabrooks who, not only participated in the initial phase of the development, but shepherded the entire project to its current form, including obtaining the publisher. Without his leadership and tenacity, the project would not have been completed.

DeRionne Pollard and Helen Benjamin served in supportive roles and assisted in a variety of ways, including working with contributors, proofreading documents, and serving as co-editors with Joe in a decision-making capacity. Thanks are extended as well to Linda Cerruti who knew the power of 100 words.

There would be no book without the contributions of the 18 members who share their stories and experiences in this volume. Their participation and support are greatly appreciated.

Finally, the entire membership is owed a debt of gratitude for their support of our organization through the years.

Dedication

This book is dedicated to 30 African-American community college CEOs across the United States who had the foresight in 1983 to pay forward their experiences, insights, and knowledge for future generations of African-American community college CEOs to reap the benefits. They built the foundation, paved the way, and established the pipeline ensuring opportunity for growth and development of highly resourceful leaders. Their dedication and commitment have become the pillars anchoring a mighty platform on which today's leaders stand to promote and advocate on behalf of all African-American students, faculty, staff, and administrators.

Today, tomorrow, and for decades to come, African-American CEOs will pass the torch lit by this outstanding group of CEOs. The Presidents' Round Table will forever remain vibrant and steady as each generation of new leaders embraces its core values, while creating new blueprints of thoughts and experiences. Tests for leadership strengths will occur, yet many leaders will prevail with true professionalism out of respect of the shoulders upon which they stand. We thank them for lighting that torch and creating the Presidents' Round Table and laying the foundation for the development of this anthology.

1983 Presidents' Round Table Officers
Dr. Charles A. Green, *Convener*
Dr. Freddie Nicholas, *Secretary*
Dr. Vernon Crawley, *Treasurer*

1983 Presidents' Round Table Members

Ewin Akin
Earl Bowman
Ezekiel Bryant
Mattie Bryant
Dr. Constance Carroll
Dr. Leadie Clark
Dr. Carl M. Crawford
Dr. Nolen Ellison
Dr. Homer Franklin

Dr. Donald Godbold
Dr. Robert T. Green
John Greene
Dr. James Griggs
Johnny Harris
Dr. Zelema Harris
Dr. Odell Johnson
Dr. Yvonne Kennedy
Dr. Wright Lassiter
Dr. Ralph Lee

Dr. Donald Phelps
Dr. Roy Phillips
Dr. Queen Randall
Dr. Abel Sykes
Dr. Lionel Sylvas
Dr. Richard Turner
Dr. Rosetta Wheaton
Dr. Zachary Yamba

The Chocolate Truth

an anthology of perspectives from community college CEOs

Presented by the Presidents' Round Table
A Collaboration of African American Community College Chief
Executive Officers

Project Editor: Joe Seabrooks, Ph.D.
Project Co-Editors: Helen Benjamin Pd.D.
De Rionne P. Pollard Ph.D.

Published By
My Vision Works Publishing
Farmington Hills, MI 48334

The Presidents' Round Table

About the Presidents' Round Table

The Presidents' Round Table was founded in January 1983 to bring together African American community college chief executive officers for the purpose of ensuring their success as campus leaders. The group initially focused on advocacy for each other and mentorships to ensure African American legacy in campus leadership positions. Other priorities included successful matriculation of African American students and employment opportunities for African Americans in community colleges across the nation with special emphasis on grooming future presidents.

Founding Officers

Convener: Dr. Charles A. Green
President, Maricopa Technical Community College, Phoenix, Arizona

Secretary: Dr. Freddie Nicholas
President, J. Sergeant Reynolds Community College, Richmond, Virginia

Treasurer: Dr. Vernon Crawley
President, Forest Park Community College, St. Louis, Missouri

Past Conveners

Dr. Charles A. Green Dr.
Richard Turner, III
Dr. Earl Bowman
Dr. Eileen Baccus
Dr. Roy Phillips
Dr. Belle Wheelan
Dr. Jack E. Daniels, III
Dr. Janis Hadley
Dr. Charles A. Taylor

Current Officers

Convener: Dr. Helen Benjamin
Chancellor, Contra Costa Community College District

Secretary: Dr. Andrew C. Jones
Chancellor, Coast Community College District

Treasurer: Dr. Thelma Scott-Skillman
President, Folsom Lake College

Membership Chair: Dr. Ken Atwater
President, Hillsborough Community College

Lakin Institute Coordinator: Dr. Charlene Dukes
President, Prince George's Community College

Introduction

The Presidents' Round Table of African American Community College CEOs, an outgrowth of the National Council on Black American Affairs, was established in 1983 by 30 members holding CEO leadership positions across the United States. In the ensuing 29 years, that number has grown to 110. The organization continues to meet the original purpose of ensuring the success of its members as college leaders.

The initial focus was on advocacy for each other and mentorships to support the African American legacy in community college leadership positions. Other priorities included a focus on successful matriculation of African American students and identifying employment opportunities for African Americans in community colleges across the nation with a special emphasis on grooming future presidents.

Through the years, the goals of the organization have been met through a variety of activities planned in the annual business meetings and professional development activities for the membership. In addition, the Thomas Lakin Institute for Mentored Leadership has been conducted by the Round Table since 1994 for those who aspire to the presidency. More than 275 African-Americans in senior leadership positions have benefitted from participation in the Institute since its inception.

This anthology grew out of the desire to support the current membership in a more tangible and lasting way--in the expression of real life experiences through the medium of the story.

As we discussed the project, we pondered two questions. Whom do we want to tell our story? Is our story valuable enough to be told? To the former question, we responded that we must tell our own story; to the latter, most definitely! Too often, African American stories have been devalued by us as well as others. As a consequence, many stories from our ancestors went to their graves with them, silenced forever. *The Chocolate Truth* is a collaborative storytelling project that ensures such an ignominious omission will not be repeated. This powerful collection of narratives is an undertaking that transfers the wisdom of the elders from one generation to another.

Today's African American community college chief executive officers and other senior managers across America tell their individual stories and experiences in their own words. What was their career path? What were the underlying values that sustained them through the challenges on their journey? Who encouraged them? These stories, some painful, others humorous, will teach, inspire and leave a legacy for another generation to follow in their footsteps.

Dispersed by geography, the voices speaking from these pages may at times seem isolated and unsupported. However, as an organizational community, we share a profound understanding of our collective identity. That understanding strengthens us as we endeavor to reshape colleges for student success in the twenty-first century. These contributors are modern day griots. Alex Haley said, "When a griot dies, a library has burned to the ground." *The Chocolate Truth* is a trove of black history, and through the sharing of these stories and experiences, we have broken the cycle of silence. The library remains intact.

The Chocolate Truth:

an anthology of perspectives from college CEOs

Presented by The Presidents' Round Table

 # PART ONE

FITTING IN

The Joy Is in the Journey

The Right Fit at the Right Time

Eagerness Won't Break Dawn

1

THE JOY IS IN THE JOURNEY

I began my career as an educator at the tender age of 21, teaching in a newly racially integrated public high school in the South. Since then, I've worked at a historically Black institution and at community colleges in teaching and administrative positions. Because of my long tenure in education, I tend to think of my career in academic rather than calendar years. The 1989-90 academic year stands out as a turning point in my life — a year in which I made a decision that changed my life. In search of new challenges, I left the safety and comfort of a place where I had spent 22 years with friends, family, as well as numerous former students and colleagues. I had an opportunity to move to the West, and I did so to the astonishment of just about everyone I knew. Uprooting my life and my family for a job showed me just how much my personal and professional lives were intertwined.

Because I was a single mother, I took great care in preparing for the move. I made two advance visits to check out neighborhoods, schools, and churches in the area of the college where I was to work. My children were in junior high and high school at the time, so I interviewed principals and toured several schools in order to determine which community would best suit our needs. I moved ahead of the children so that everything would be in place when they arrived. I rented a house that just happened to have a swimming pool, hoping that would ease the transition for my children.

Not only did I plan for my family, but I also felt mentally prepared for what I would find in my new job. Prior to accepting the new position, I had served in four different work environments and had adjusted very well to each of them. In my mind, this move would not be different. I had done my homework and knew what the major differences were between the environment I was leaving and the new frontier. The "from" and "to" issues were very clear to me. I was moving from a right-to-work state to one with collective bargaining; from an environment in which shared governance was often practiced to an environment in which it was legislated; and from a state where students had responsibility for their tuition to one where the state had a history of funding tuition for all students enrolled in community colleges.

My first month on the job was in July when the campus was very quiet, which was a good time to acclimate. As a new administrator, my first act was to send a letter of introduction to all of the employees with whom I would be working directly. The letter took people by surprise. One faculty member showed up in my office to see a manager who would be open and brave enough to do such a thing. For me, it was just the normal thing to do. That faculty member's reaction could've been more about her than the rest of the folks, but there was a lesson in her reaction. Her visit to my office was the first in a litany of clues that set me off, leading me to think that maybe I had missed something in my research and planning activities. I wanted to hold a meeting with everyone in my division but was advised against it. As an educator, I believed in using my skills and talents to make a difference in the lives of students. I began to sense a difference between my educational philosophy and my new environment, but I still was at a point where I believed I could overcome cultural differences. I realized, however, that the transition wouldn't be as easy as I had hoped.

My children arrived in the second month. Once I saw them in this new environment, any lingering hope of a smooth transition was completely shattered. We knew no one in the area. We had each other, and that was it. We moved from a thriving large city with a prosperous Black community to a small bedroom community and the contrasts were startling. I'll never forget my son's reaction as I drove them to our new home from the airport. As we passed the display with the insignias of the various service clubs attached, he said, "Mama, where are you taking us? This has to be a small town with signs like that." And that swimming pool I mentioned did not help. The house was on a hill; most days during the summer the wind was so high that the pool was unusable. Many nights, the wind would blow the water against the back of the house, making it difficult to sleep.

My children began school in the third month. They made friends fairly easily, but both missed their old friends and our family terribly. I made a commitment that we would not go back for a year because I knew that if we left our new home for a visit to the old one, we probably wouldn't return. By the fourth month, we were in family therapy dealing with our adjustment issues. During these first few months, the immortal words of Robert Burns haunted me:

PART ONE: FITTING IN

The best laid plans of mice men
Often go awry,
And leave us nothing but grief and pain
For promised joy.

I had tried to plan for everything, but there are some things for which plans cannot be made. I couldn't adequately plan for how each of us would feel in the new environment. Yes, I had the logistics down to a science. Everything went as planned; some of it even seemed divinely inspired. But the bottom line was simple: All three of us were miserable. However, I couldn't show it, especially not at home. I maintained my optimism and good spirits at home and at work. But in the sixth month, I began a mad search for a job anywhere in the South. I had no choice; I had to get us out. I hit a wall of doubt and panic, wondering what I had done and why it hadn't gone perfectly.

I made it my goal to have a new a new job by the next academic year. I applied for at least six jobs and did not get one interview. I used every connection I had to no avail. In the meantime, the three of us trudged along. I learned more about my new job and community, and my children assimilated into the new community against their respective wills. We looked forward to our weekly counseling sessions at Rainbow Psychotherapy. My children fondly referred to our counselor as the Rainbow Man. He helped us tremendously. Despite the goal I had established for myself, I did not have a new job at the end of the academic year. However, the three of us were feeling whole, not completely happy, but whole. We had all made some friends and became active participants at our respective schools. I made it my new goal to find a job in the South by the end of my second academic year. Out of necessity, I had reached a point where I felt okay about staying for one more year.

Although my plan was still to spend no more than two years in this new job, I became more active at the college and served on a district committee. I maintained strict confidentiality about my search for a job. I was fully engaged at work and simultaneously looking for almost any job. The people at the college embraced my children and me, inviting us to events in the surrounding community and in their homes. Yet I was still finding it difficult to adjust to the new environment where managers had practically no voice; where most citizens felt that they should make no personal financial investment in their education because of a promise the state made to them in better financial times; and where employees seemed more interested in their wages than improvements in their working conditions. It was an environment in which students seemed secondary to me, but not to others for whom these ideas were part of their culture. There was very little innovation; any undesignated new money was expected to increase salaries. I felt I had no impact and was in a place antithetical to my educational philosophy. I had become part of a culture I did not understand and while I needed to try, I was not willing. I was firm about the two-year deadline as I entered my second year.

At some point early in that second year, the district hired a new and well-connected chancellor who left messages with my assistant that he wanted to talk to me. I couldn't believe the chancellor was calling me and therefore didn't return his calls. He eventually caught me at my desk and requested a meeting. I, of course, met with him. The first words out of his mouth were, "I hear you are trying to leave the District." Imagine my surprise! He proceeded to inform me about some opportunities at the district office that might be of interest to me. He suggested that I consider staying; he said I could help him change things. I left that meeting a bit perplexed. What had just happened? I had a plan. Who was this person and who did he think he was? Entering my life as though he had a right to be in the midst of my business. I had never seen this man in my life. But the most important question of all was: How had he found out I was trying to leave?

After that meeting, I continued my work with great zeal and assiduousness. Jobs in the South were not forthcoming. I even tried to return to my prior district, but there were no openings. I felt stuck, yet found myself, after 19 months, applying and being selected for a position at the district office.

Although I had never worked away from the learning environment, I adjusted well to the district office. My new supervisor — the chancellor who had delved too deeply into my business — was a workhorse with a new idea every five minutes. Of course, he expected me to execute every one of these ideas. I became immersed in the new job and worked harder than ever, eventually growing to enjoy the responsibilities and opportunities offered. Not only did the new job improve my knowledge and experience in community colleges, but it also strengthened my ability to work with others, expanded my network within and outside the district, and enhanced my management skills. I also found that this new position changed my perspective on the district. I became willing to learn and accept the new culture, and realized I could have an impact, small though it may be. With all these changes, my desire to leave dissipated.

When my second year ended, I had fulfilled my goal of having a different job. However, it was only eight miles from the job I had been trying to escape, not 1,800 miles away. I suppose I got what I desired: a job that challenged me, and one in which I made a difference. That second year also ended with my son graduating from high school and heading back to his beloved

South and my daughter ready for her last year of junior high school. Things had leveled out somewhat, and we were more comfortable. It was not exactly the promised joy I had imagined, but we managed to make it the right fit for us. I have to agree with those who say the joy is in the journey, and what a journey it has been.

My son, now 36 years old, recently commented that he hated the experience at the time but grew to appreciate it as time passed. In the two years he spent in the West, he was exposed to people, ideas, and cultural phenomena he would never have experienced had we not made the move.

Incredibly, he speaks of that period as a time of enlightenment. My daughter eventually flourished in the environment, having now become a permanent resident. She had fully acclimated by the time she became a senior in high school. She realized on a visit back home that she no longer fit in there — she was very different from those she had longed to be with. She does want to go home, but only to visit. For me, it's been 21 years since I moved, and I am in the same community college district serving in my sixth position. One of those positions was as interim president of the college where I was first hired. In the intervening years, I have become stronger and better. Like my son, I realize I am a different person than I would have been had I not made the move. What certainly seemed like a wrong fit in the beginning turned out to be quite all right, and I like the person I have become as a result.

2

THE RIGHT FIT AT THE RIGHT TIME

Within the context of African American popular culture in my lifetime, I have witnessed some of the most ridiculous fads in the history of the world. Do you remember the days when we made biker shorts, polyester suits, and bell-bottom pants popular? How about our embrace of hairstyles like the Jheri Curl or the high-top fade? Even in contemporary Black America, we are obsessed with fads like tattoos, piercings, and, yes – skinny jeans.

One of my favorite things to do in the entire world is convince my colleagues to share images and photos of themselves from back in the day. If you ever need a foolproof icebreaker, just ask your executive board or your cabinet to submit photos of themselves at ages 18 or 21. Nothing breaks the ice like going down memory lane with images from way back when, particularly if cocktails are involved during the recollection. Sharing images of our former selves allows us to be the vulnerable humans that we are and creates the potential space to build bonds that can last a lifetime.

Just as our participation in fashion fads and trends has been a part of the African American tradition for generations, I would argue that we have gravitated to careers that have been prominently promoted in the media and popular culture. Television shows and movies that fairly represented African Americans made their careers appear "cool." For example, *Julia,* the nurse character portrayed by Diahann Carroll, became a professional role model for many black women. Blair Underwood's character, Jonathan Rollin, on *LA Law,* had many brothers wanting to go to law school, and Malik Yoba's part in *New York Undercover* had many of us thinking that being a detective could be cool if we could bring our own flavor and style to the job.

My generation—Generation X, born between 1965 and 1980—came of age with films like *School Daze* and *Higher Learning,* and the popular television show *A Different World,* all of which portrayed the black "baby boomer" higher education professional. As a result, many of us got the notion that we could serve at the level of CEO. These seeds of leadership ambition were often planted and nurtured by the black "boomers" in our profession. Therefore, it is no surprise that many in my generation and younger generations aspire to ascend to the highest level of post-secondary leadership. This relatively new professional trend is wonderful, to some degree. Serving students with the goal of advancing humanity is a remarkable gesture and an honorable aspiration. However, most young professionals don't have a clue with regard to what it really means to take on this type of accountability. I have had the privilege of visiting with brothers and sisters all across the country. I have also mentored folks whose current positions run the gamut: from the first-year graduate student working on a master's in higher education administration to the individual who has been serving the profession for more than ten years. In doing so, I have observed that most are pursuing the position of college CEO without really being clear why they should. When I ask, "Why do you want to be a college president or college CEO?" they often respond, "Because it is an important role, and I think it is a good fit for me." Yet, most really do not know what it truly means to be a president, both personally and professionally.

※ Why the Presidency?

When I entered my first and current position as a college president, I was extremely naïve. To be completely honest, I had absolutely no idea what I was getting myself into upon accepting the role as a community college CEO. I have frequently been caught off guard by what some of my dearest colleagues and friends have eloquently labeled "the human factor." We should be experts in the "human factor," considering that our entire career is grounded in work serving humans, right? Sounds simple, but what I have learned over the years as a campus CEO is that things are never as simple as they might appear. That is primarily because people believe that most of the authority and decision-making on college matters are ultimately left to my discretion.

The human factor often shows up when an individual who has been given authority (vice presidents, deans, division chairs, etc.) makes an unpopular decision. An inevitable response is that a handful of individuals who have historically received favor will often proceed to have what many in the Southern language tradition would label a "fit." Now, for those who don't know what a fit is, please allow me to break it down for you: As a child, like most children, I struggled with learning how to manage my emotions. Any little thing would set me off, whether it was going to bed or losing a kickball game. My Grandma, God rest her soul, defined a fit as The devil's temporary hold on my babies." Then she would explain how necessary it was to take a belt or a switch to beat the hell and the "devil" out of you.

By my own definition, fits are Temporary Moments of Insanity (TMOI). No one is immune to TMOI, and I am talking about students, staff, faculty, community members, and board members. TMOI make being a college president an interesting endeavor. The ability to *respond* to TMOI, or fits, in a responsible and calm way is, from my perspective, a skill that I had no idea I needed in addressing "the human factor." Responding to TMOI is a skill that's critical to perfect, if at all possible. When you choose to accept a presidency, you are choosing a lifestyle, a lifestyle where people are constantly going to have fits. I play so many roles, it's often difficult to even identify them. One minute I can be a mediator, the next minute a coach, then turn around and be a judge. Often times, I believe I'm a surrogate parent. I console people while giving them bad news, then pat others on the back for a job well done. Sometimes I'm not sure whether I'm home with my two boys and lovely bride or at work. I spend a great deal of time helping people work through TMOI.

On any given day, you can find yourself pulled in twenty different directions. In the same conversation, you can find yourself involved in meaningful and constructive matters as well as some that address absolutely ridiculous and silly issues. You may be having an email exchange about your strategy to get a $25 million grant, only to be interrupted by someone who wants to know why they can't find a parking space. Some of the things presidents have to deal with are absolutely frivolous and utterly ridiculous.

Most of us possess tools and technology that make our jobs less difficult to balance. We typically will have an iPhone, Blackberry, Treo, or some type of communication device that keeps us connected twenty-four hours a day, seven days a week to people and things that require our attention. In all seriousness, it is sad, but the presidency is an anti-family position. If you're an individual who values time with your significant other or spouse, or if you're a person who wants to be active in your children's lives, you have to be very strategic and intentional about all of these roles. It is a difficult balance and most of us fail most of the time. And if you are not of the temperament to effectively deal with people having TMOI on a constant basis, you might want to re-think the presidency.

✠   Chasing Purpose

From my personal perspective, identifying one's purpose is, unequivocally, the most important thing a person can do. We are in an unprecedented time in history when there are very few professions and industries to which those who look like us have not gained access. Not only are we represented, but, in many cases, we are present at the highest levels. In the vast majority of professions, African Americans have successfully laid the ground work or drafted the successful blueprint. In most instances, these trailblazers who have come before us are committed to helping other blacks gain access by mentoring and coaching. In many cases, because we are convinced all things are possible, professionally, we are often distracted and struggle to navigate our very noisy professional and personal spaces.

What quiets all the noise, helps me focus, and keeps me on track is being able to fall back on my purpose. In some cases, however, it's almost laughable when I talk to others about the subject. Most of us have no idea what our purpose is or why we should define it. Often times when I ask people, "What is your purpose?" they mostly reflect on what I call temporary states of the human condition. Let me give you a few examples: The most popular definition of purpose that I hear from people, young and young at heart, deals with having a high quality of life, a decent standard of living, and/or being able to take care of a family. As admirable as these goals are, it's difficult to accept these ideas as associated with one's purpose. Clearly, it is an honorable aspiration to want to offer a quality lifestyle to your family. However, one's purpose cannot be tied to a temporary state of being. What happens when you experience things that are out of your control, such as a car accident or a life-threatening illness, and you are not able to work? All of sudden you are disabled and not in a position to provide for your family in the same fashion. How can you live your purpose, in this example, if you can't work? Do you jump off a bridge? Slit your wrists? I surely hope not.

I cannot emphasize enough that *your true purpose should not be connected to anything that can be taken away from you!* My purpose is to empower individuals who have historically been denied a higher education, and to improve the quality of life for them and their families through an outstanding collegiate experience. I am absolutely convinced I can live my purpose regardless of my life situation; whether I am a college president, professor, advisor, administrative assistant, custodian, or even unemployed, I can chase my purpose. My experiences, knowledge, and contacts will allow me to pursue my purpose regardless of how I earn a living, my marital status, physical condition, etc. I strongly suggest that you find your purpose and find ways to pursue your purpose with all the passion and energy you can gather.

✠ Know Thy Strengths

The road to the chief executive office in any industry requires individuals to amply demonstrate multiple strengths, and in many cases the constituents you serve will think you can be all things to all people. I have yet to meet an individual who has even dared to claim perfection in every way, or strength in every area. No matter how many books and articles you read or how many leadership seminars you attend, you will probably never encounter The Perfect Leader. The best leaders clearly understand their strengths and weaknesses and surround themselves with people who are strong in areas that the leaders are not. Many of us make the mistake of hiring people who are just like us, which is not wise. Understanding your strengths is not necessarily easy, but there are many tools available to help an individual identify his or her attributes. I personally prefer "Strength Quest" or "Strength Finder," an online survey that asks you a series of questions, analyzes your responses, and identifies your five primary qualities. I have used my strengths to help guide me, professionally. This process has also helped me identify people who possess the skills I do not possess, in order to maximize my own.

✠ The Legacy You Leave

The legacy I leave is absolutely the most important thing to me, personally and professionally. For the past fifteen years I have deliberately attempted to focus almost all of my energy on helping others improve their lives through higher education. For all of these years my purpose has guided my career. Whether I'm in the classroom, at a conference, in the boardroom or on the street, I make it a point to engage and help people understand how higher education works and how it can best serve them or someone they love dearly. I believe in this notion so deeply that, during interviews, I frequently say: "Let's assume you get the job. Let us fast-forward to when you're ready to move on to the next phase of your career. What will I be able to say about you at your going-away party?" This question often catches people off guard, primarily because most people pursuing a new opportunity rarely think beyond the position they are actively pursuing. My personal answer to this question is this: When my career is over and it's time for me to go on to the next phase of my life, first and foremost, I want my boss(es) to have grossly underestimated the size of the venue needed to accommodate the people who want to say goodbye to the old man. I want it said by folks from all across the globe that, at some time during their lives, I challenged them, inspired them, touched them, encouraged them, and maybe even kicked them in the rear end from time to time. It's very important to me to leave behind a professional legacy that suggests one can lead with love and make the world a better place by simply helping people reach their full potential.

Finding a Match

Finding the "right fit," situation, or professional circumstance has been like a loud and persistent drum that many of my mentors and coaches have sounded throughout my career. This is something that isn't talked about enough as we attempt to coach and mentor individuals, professionally. Nonetheless, many of us have ignored words of caution when we were fortunate enough to hear them, and succumbed to the powerful lure of financial rewards and prestige that go with landing the big job. We sometimes jump too quickly at opportunities without considering whether there's a fit with our purpose and skill set. As I've already suggested, skinny jeans ain't right for everybody – and this concept goes far beyond fashion trends; it applies to our professional choices as well. It's critical to remember that there are roughly 1,200 community colleges in our country, and not everyone can be successful in working at each and every one of them. Please don't feel like you have to leap at the first opportunity that presents itself. All you need is one institutional match, and if you prepare for it by expanding your competencies and building your network, the odds are greatly in your favor. Every campus has its own unique benefits, its own culture, and its own mystique. Be clear about the things that are important to the institution and what's important to you and to your family. My number one criterion when considering an opportunity is to find institutions where the individual(s) I report to are caring, supportive, and invested in my growth and development. There is a trick to this because, for individuals to care about you and be supportive of you, they have to know you. They have to really know what's important to you, and they have to know what makes you tick. In order for this to happen, you have to make yourself vulnerable from the very beginning, starting with the interview. You must be honest about the things that are important, such as being able to engage with students, helping them think through choices, and challenging them to work harder to become better scholars and people.

What is also very important to me is engaging African American males. I have made a personal commitment to mentor as many young black men as my obligations will allow. I am committed to making African American male academic achievement one of my highest priorities for two reasons: 1) a great deal of my success can be attributed to the host of black men who have served as role models in my life (i.e. coaches, teachers, neighbors, etc.), and; 2) nearly every indicator (i.e. GPA, retention rates, graduation, etc.) suggests that African American academic achievement is one of this country's most critical issues. Though I cannot save every brother on the planet, I can make a difference. Any institution that I serve must know that I will be engaged with African American young men and I will be soliciting the support and partnership of other positive African American male professionals. Truthfully, this is not a fit with the goals of every institution, so it's one of the first things I've shared in interviews, in order to gauge whether I'm a good match.

Also, I am a big fan of institutions with vibrant campus environments where students are thinking about the world they live in and challenging others to do the same. An environment with a rich, strong student government and tons of student organizations and student engagement opportunities is exciting to me. In addition, I very much enjoy intellectual discourse and appreciate opportunities where folks do not always agree, but know how to agree to disagree.

Clarify what's important to you. Figure out what legacy you will leave, what strengths you can rely upon, and how they connect you to your purpose and desire to pursue a presidency. The individual who is strategic and committed can find himself or herself in a community college CEO position. However, always remember: Just like biker shorts, polyester suits, bell-bottom pants, Jheri Curls, and high-top fades came and went, your goal to become a college president can change. If you decide to go for it, do so knowing you are in pursuit for the right reasons. If, while on your journey, you find that a college CEO position is the wrong destination – just like skinny jeans ain't right for everybody – you can find a better or more comfortable career track.

3

EAGERNESS WON'T BREAK DAWN FASTER

At a leadership training institute, I once said, "I know I can get a presidency. I just want to learn how to keep it." My presumption turned out to be true — I am a college president — but I had no idea what kind of journey I was embarking on. For many of us, the experience of writing a doctoral dissertation is a life-changing undertaking. While the search process is for a different purpose, it resembles in great part the process of successfully completing the dissertation. As I went through several searches, I became aware that I had been perhaps too confident about finding a presidency. I did find one, but I am still experiencing the keeping it part.

There are certainly many opportunities to learn about the search process. There are institutes sponsored by many organizations: ACCT, AACC, the Presidents' Round Table, Lakin Institute, etc. Availing oneself of as many of them as possible is a wonderful opportunity. While none of them will get you the presidency, they make the road to it less thorny and can give you much insight into the job itself.

So, you're preparing to become a CEO of a community college. What will it take to get you there? What will your initial year be like? How do you ensure a successful transition from the peaceful life of a vice president or dean into the turbulent and wacky world of the head of an institution? I will share my perspective with you and hope you will join me soon as a CEO or first-year college president, as I hopefully enter my second year, still employed at the same institution.

Planting the Seed

I can't recall the first time I thought or said out loud that it would be a good idea to become a college president. What I do know is that I went through several phases and while I gave up the idea many times, it returned again and again over a 10-year period. Holding secondary school credentials, I wanted at first to be a superintendent of schools, to be at the top of my profession. When I began my studies in the higher education program at the University of Kansas and later was hired as Director of Academic and Student Affairs at Duluth Community College, I quickly decided that presidency at the college level was my goal. I never gave myself a timeline for when I would become president. I quickly learned that it was not something I could rush, but rather it was something I grew into.

Attempt Number One

Prior to my first application for presidency, I served as acting Director/President of the Duluth Community College Center. I took the position during a turbulent time, when the college was preparing to merge with Duluth Technical College to form Lake Superior College. My role in the merger helped boost my confidence and belief that I was able to progress beyond the dean's position I had obtained only a few months earlier. Four or five years later, I heard about a presidency in the Midwest. It was my first application. Looking back on it, I am surprised that I even heard back from the institution, but I got a small bite. I must have made it out of the first reading by the search committee. A member of the board called me to do some follow-up on my experience. He kindly said that my community involvement was inadequate for what the college was looking for. Although as a Dean and Vice President I had a pretty good history of community collaboration, my experience was not enough to be presidential.

This first exclusion taught me that, in order to advance, I needed to be more meaningfully involved in the community. My involvement with the school district and the local university was positive, but there was a much larger world out there to impact as a community leader. Without that, the road to the presidency would be rocky.

Many Attempts In Vain

I applied for another presidency at a large community college campus in the Midwest. I received a call from the search consultant, who shared that I was on the list of options. He was encouraging and asked that I not be discouraged in light of my track record. I listened to him and applied for a few more presidencies as I was simultaneously applying for a lateral move. The lateral worked out very well. I became Chief Academic Officer (CAO) and nearly swore that I would retire in the position along with my boss. The presidency sounded too risky, and as CAO I was closer to the students than I would've been as president. Just as I put the idea to rest, colleagues and friends started to overtly encourage my attempt at the presidency. At that point I began to attend institutes and seminars about the presidency, which opened my eyes. I realized that I hadn't always been ready but was on my way to acquiring the necessary skills to become not just a candidate, but also a contender.

The first institute was a half-day workshop that acquainted me with the position and gave me some insight into what institutions are looking for and how to match my skills with the advertised position. The best part was getting to know the search firms and what they are, and are not able to do. I was elated to join the mailing lists of some firms. I thought that as long as the announcement came to me, I was able to apply for the position. After a few rejections, it occurred to me that I shouldn't go after all positions. I started refining my reading of the ads and began to pick and choose what I would venture into. The other important part of the institute for me was the relationships I built with other professionals that developed into strong friendships and inseparable bonds. These relationships would later serve as a major support while I persevered in the search process.

I attended a second training where, for the first time, I faced reality and matured into a future president. This particular institute ripped my résumé apart and helped me to rebuild it from the ground up. Because of the massive job of rebuilding, I spent almost two years in hiatus and didn't express interest in any vacancies. During that time, I became thoroughly immersed in the community. I became chair of some important boards and engaged the community with the college and the college with the community. These activities were not just résumé -builders, but also helped me to understand what it means to be the leader in a community when your college is one of the greatest resources it has. I learned to realistically engage a board and a committee in discussions that were fruitful. The vain attempts at a new position helped me to realize that when I did finally make it to the next position, I would, if I had my way, be the CEO for the rest of my career.

✠ Moving Up From the Inside

Along this road called life many things can happen. You find yourself with an opportunity, but you dare not take it. As our president retired, I felt tempted to go for it. By then, I had decided that I wanted to remain a VP and had too many things to accomplish at the college to leave. Although I had many months to think about the position, I was in no hurry, and finally concluded that I did not want to apply to replace my boss. He had done a tremendous job and his legacy needed to be kept intact. I thought that I could do better as the Chief Academic Officer. We had formed a great team, the best cabinet I had worked with, and things were going pretty well. We even had money to get things done. Only a few people encouraged me to apply. It didn't matter how many came though, I was not going to change my mind. My résumé was probably a good six months from being ready to go.

While many vice presidents successfully take over the presidency, for many VPs it hasn't been a good move. I didn't know what would happen to me, and I didn't want to know because there was no interest on my part to lead that fine institution our cabinet had transformed. I was curious to see what someone else would do when she/he accepted this challenge. Would the person maintain the stability we had known or move us in a different direction? Completely annihilate the progress of the past seven years and bring us back to where we were before? Or take what we were and make us an even better institution? We still had a few missing pieces to be an elite institution. The curiosity was too much for me not to want to see what would happen next.

My curiosity led me to violate two principles I had held dear. If you are the vice president for academic affairs and your president leaves, you should pack your bag and hand the incoming president the keys as she's coming in. I have observed too many vice presidents' fates be handed to them by an incoming president, but then I was confident that my job was secure because of the team we had in place. Few people would come in and dissolve such a diverse and high-producing team. We got along better than most cabinets I had known. The second previously held principle was that I would not serve on the search committee for the presidency and would avoid being nominated to the committee. In this case when I was asked whether I would be on the committee, I decided that the best choice was to join the committee to hire my new boss. I thought that vice presidents who are candidates at their own institutions often do not survive the new administration, if they do not become the president. By being on the committee, it left no doubt to outstanding candidates that this CAO was not a competitor. I faithfully served on the committee and was able to sit on the other side of the table from a presidential candidate. I enjoyed the role and learned much from it.

I've never regretted not applying. The college hired a veteran president who found a way to move the college in a new direction. I learned many lessons from behind the curtain about institutional fit, the power of the board, the role of the search consultant, the swings of committees, and how to seem succinct and presidential in the interview process.

The Successful Attempt

There is a Haitian proverb, "Twò prese pa fè jou louvri." It translates to, "Being eager won't break dawn faster." Things take their own time, and they happen when they're supposed to. Forcing them does not guarantee better or faster results. Some candidates get their presidency on their first try. I haven't seen any statistics to know what the numbers are, but many of us tried multiple times before it happened. Perhaps we weren't mature or polished enough, and the long process helped shape us for presidency. Having fellow candidates to compare notes with is a great morale booster, and making the search process a team effort makes it more bearable.

My résumé was re-polished and ready to go. I was feeling more and more comfortable in my position with a new president on board. I could see staying in place for another three years. It would make it more apparent that I was a stable person, despite the fact that I had gone all over the country for my career: Kansas, Minnesota, Maryland, and Nevada. Granted I had been at the same place for almost seven years, so a move would have been acceptable. The longer you stay, the harder it may be to leave. As things started to take shape with a new president and a new agenda, however, the thought of moving on became more appealing.

I was feeling more and more confident and it became time to search for the right fit. In this search process and when the search firms know you, the announcements can be attractive. There may be times when a consultant knows your characteristics and feels that you're the right fit for an institution. Then it may really be time to listen, even if you're not sure about the institution or your experience. The matter of suitability cannot be over- emphasized. Sometimes the candidate and the institution are simply not the right fit for one another. As humans, our tendency may be to adjust and adapt. There is just so much adaptation and adjustment that can happen until the president and the institution are torn apart. Barbara Tuchman wrote in The March of Folly of, "...acting according to wish while not allowing oneself to be deflected by the facts." There is no real barometer to determine precisely whether new leadership will or will not work.

A consultant recruited me for my current position, but I had my doubts. The consultant worked with me to convince me that it could work. She explained to me that the interpersonal skills she believed I had were exactly what was needed at the college. Though the institution had suffered from instability and other neglects, I was told there were early signs that it could recover. As a candidate, you need to build trust with a consultant before you can accept what he or she is telling you. A consultation will not necessarily translate into a presidential contract. While serving on the search committee at my previous institution, I learned that the consultant's power is limited. There were decisions we made in the absence of the consultant. After all, the role of the consultant ends at some point, and the college and its president will need to embrace each other.

Switching from the personality of a vice president or dean to president takes a lot of practice, self-discipline, and a focus on the job ahead. It also requires an understanding of the job being applied for and not necessarily the job one wants or will ultimately hold a year or two down the road. The institution evolves with the new CEO and changes for better or worse. Unless you're entering a very stable situation or you're moving up from within the institution, it is likely that new paradigms will be created from both a ready institution and a willing president.

Consultants will tell you to "Be presidential in your interviews." You're not applying for the VP of student services or the VP of academic affairs or the VP for finance and administration. Switching roles takes a lot of practice, self-discipline, and a focus on the job ahead. It also requires that one understand the job being applied for and not necessarily the job one wants or will ultimately hold a year or two down the road. The institution evolves with the new CEO and changes for better or worse. Unless you're entering a very stable presidency from within the institution, it's likely that new paradigms will be created and new opportunities will emerge from both a ready institution and a willing president.

⚑ The Presidency: Year One

For myself, the physical move into presidency ended up being a good step. The presidency in and of itself is something unique. Too many first-year presidents have been too busy to write the perfect book to let those who are coming up know to tighten their seatbelts for the turbulence ahead or to remind more experienced presidents where they were before they were presidents.

⊠ First Actions

Once hired, there are certain institutional issues that you must address relatively quickly. In my case, accreditation was an issue, and the relationship with the accreditation commission needed attention. Therefore, the day after my selection I went to meet with the president of the commission. As I had learned in previous position, interaction with the community is key and so I quickly addressed the college's lack of presence in the community. We focused on all communities and areas that contribute to the college funding. At the same time, we focused on building internal relationships with different groups and individuals without allowing any one group to feel disenfranchised. For example, I immediately addressed a previously unacknowledged scheduling request from the night cleaning crew. My thought was if I could listen to the night cleaning crew, who are invisible to the college community, I will surely be able to connect with the colleagues who I see regularly, and hear their issues.

⊠ The First Faculty and Staff Meeting

What should one say at the first all-college meeting? To answer this question was more difficult even than preparation for the presidential interview. Since the open forum as a candidate, the faculty meeting is the first time the college hears the president. This topic was never addressed in any institutes about presidency that I attended. I found out what all new presidents learned: The first all-college meeting is a time to set out some broad goals about the direction of the institution, taking into account the current culture, the challenges being faced, and where the community would like to see you. It's also a time to share globally what you've heard from different constituents. For your first speech, there is no map telling you where exactly to go. It's wide open.

Using some tricks of my own and some I learned along the way, I crafted a special first address to the college community that was well received and that I try to live up to daily. I preceded the speech by giving recognition to some of our hardest-working people. These were individuals I got to know during my first few days as hard workers, whose work is respected by all: the payroll clerk who had worked cheerfully and extremely hard without the support of good software to meet payroll deadlines, the faculty member who took on additional duties to look after a group of African American students with the prospect of not being funded, the co-chairs of the accreditation report who helped us to move to probation from show-cause. I wanted to, at the very start, improve relations between the unions and administration. Prior to the speech, I called every union president as well as the academic senate president on stage and handed each of them an olive branch as a symbol of my new administration's willingness to work with them in harmony to advance the college. Once the hearts of many of my colleagues were melted — or so I hoped — I proceeded to deliver a few remarks that were peppered with humor along the way. There was one quote that I used and continue to use when I make presentations to the community. It's by Laurence J. Peter: "You can always tell a real friend: when you've made a fool of yourself, he doesn't feel you've done a permanent job." I surmised that the faculty and staff needed to reconnect with the positive aspects of the college and that prior administrations had caused issues. I hoped, through these broad strokes, to bring about universal forgiveness. Unfortunately, the universality of the forgiveness did not materialize, as we still had individuals who were affected by the reorganization I had proposed and were not pleased with the potential loss of jobs for their colleagues of many years.

Everybody on the Bus

Always remember that your end-goal is a well-functioning organization and one that provides the best opportunities for learning. To reach your goal, you must create a vision that everyone can buy into and move on with. If changes are necessary, it's important to determine how much reorganization the institution can embrace in one swoop. You can only truly get a sense of how much an institution is ready for through a willingness to carefully listen to constituents and the board. It's important to write down promises, to scan the landscape and evaluate resources to move the institution in the desired direction at the comfortable pace for the institution. Changes that involve expending new resources are obviously more difficult to implement. Restructuring to meet new demands seems to be acceptable, but will nevertheless run into opposition. The opposition will show up regardless of the route you take. Inaction will also be evaluated unfavorably. Of course, acting for the sake of acting is not wise. However, you cannot lose sight of your goal.

Leading your college towards success is a difficult project that will be realized through goals, accomplishments, mentoring, and training. In my current position, we endeavor to hold retreats on these issues, to evaluate on the principles of an effective and humane organization, and to develop a culture of managerial accountability for the wellness of the employees.

✠ Don't Rush Dawn

Being a CEO is one of the last rungs on the ladder of the college hierarchy and as such should not be rushed. The fall from the presidency is daunting and near fatal. Many presidents have recovered from the precipice. Many have not recovered, and it often means the end of a great career for which the president might have worked for many years. It also means a major disappointment for the college where hundreds of people were vested in a search that resulted in a less than perfect match. The Haitian proverb I cited earlier rings true here. Don't rush it; it's best to wait until you've gained years of experience.

As I was going through the search process for my current position, I felt more and more drawn into the institution. By the time the search was over and I was the chosen candidate, I felt that this could be and will be my home for the remainder of my career. I say this because I truly believe that the college deserves a long-term serving president and I can fill that need as I strive daily to develop into a better president. While I had publicly stated my sentiment of commitment, I had no idea how well received my promise would be to the college and media. At first, I thought it was my personality that caused people to embrace my commitment. As I discovered later, it was simply because the college had had four presidents in the span of two years and stability was necessary in the administrative building. I learned to appreciate that it is not about me; it is about the institution, its students, its staff, and its quality faculty.

✠ Recommendations

In the end, your path towards a college presidency or otherwise will be your own, dependent on your strengths and weaknesses, abilities, and circumstances. For those applicants in need of advice, I offer the following: the first application may not be your best, but you will not know that until later; as long as you're still employed, there will always be time to ascend to the presidency; don't strive simply to become president, but more importantly to remain president; never fear your weaknesses; attend to your blind spot; seek help and mentorship from fellow presidents, and college administrators; develop trusting relationships with your colleagues and employees; and finally, develop a true love for the institution that honors you as its chief executive officer. It's an important distinction you should wear with proud.

❖ Part Two

WHO'S THAT LADY

Woman in a Man's World

Leading as an African American Woman

A Woman's Work: Managing the Profession and Taking Care of Family

4

WOMAN IN A MAN'S WORLD

Can you lead like a lady and be respected like a man? For me, the immediate answer to this question is probably, "No!"

There are major differences in the interactions between men and women, and almost everyone acknowledges these differences. Years ago, John Gray published his best-seller Men Are from Mars, Women Are from Venus, in which he talks about how to improve our relationships. He starts with the basic premise that we have different natures that can be used for mutual benefit, and he concludes by suggesting that love generally changes over time, but that relations can grow stronger and fuller with time.

While I don't mean to say that the workplace will be a love fest, I do think that, over time, relationships can mature, and if women stay the course by using effective leadership, employees will give the same respect to women that they give men. I also think they will give women the same opportunities to earn their respect. If author John Gray's premise that women and men are as different as the planets is accepted, it still leaves room for the basic question of how to handle differences in the amount of respect given to the sexes. Is there a real difference, or is it something that women see through a different lens? Does it have anything to do with our culture and how children are taught to respect their parents?

Perhaps it's rooted in the fact that many children grow up with their mothers telling them, "Just wait until your dad gets home. You're going to get it!" Do children inherently grow up thinking that they must respect men more than women because the consequences of any action they take will be less harsh when meted out by a woman? And when the consequences are about the same, do they see women as being harsher? In other words, did we as women give away our right to discipline and enforce?

When cultural conditioning is added to the fact that women are different from men and tend to act differently than men do, there is a great likelihood that biases will creep in, even where people don't intend it. These biases come from both men and women, but perhaps more so from men. Both sexes often view women in leadership roles as being difficult to work with, or to work for, and both sexes are much more likely to disagree with, or even defy, a woman in authority. When given a choice, both men and women say they prefer to work for a man; that women are less fair when disciplining an employee, and that women are "moody." In spite of my own sister's apparent love and respect for me, she doesn't hesitate to say that she never wants a "woman boss." Most women already know where we stand in this arena and are not surprised when these thoughts and biases surface in our workplace.

The "Work & Power Survey" conducted by *Elle* magazine and MSNBC.com in March 2007 suggests that stereotypes about sex and leadership are alive and well: The poll included 60,000 respondents, more than half of whom said a person's sex makes no difference in leadership capabilities, but most of whom, when expressing a preference, said men are more likely to be effective leaders. Among male respondents, 41 percent said men are more likely to be good leaders, and 33 percent of women agreed. Three out of four women who expressed a preference said they would rather work for a man than for a woman. The survey also found a bonanza of stereotypes among those polled, with many using the optional "comment" section to label women "moody," "bitchy," "gossipy," and "emotional." But the most popular term for woman – used 347 times – was "catty."

Research conducted by Jessica Selasky throughout the 1990s indicates that both men and women respect women less. She found that when asked to list three great communicators, rarely did men or women put a woman on their list. Additionally, when asked about preference in a boss, 75 percent of respondents, both men and women, said they'd rather have a man (my sister could have been one of those surveyed). According to a study of average employees, conducted by Leanne Atwater at Arizona State University West, the only thing worse than being reprimanded at work is being reprimanded by a woman. She also found that employees who were disciplined by women were more likely to believe their discipline was unfair.

In exploring differences in the workplace, Barbara Annis and Associates, Inc. facilitated over 2,000 gender awareness workshops during which women said they are dismissed, tested, treated as the "third sex," and often excluded from important opportunities to bond with the professional team. These challenges are faced on a daily basis.

✠ Dismissed

Recently, I was participating in a very high-level meeting with my partners in a private business venture. We were in the midst of a heated discussion where we were required to take actions that some partners didn't support. There had been a prolonged debate about whether we were, indeed, going to be required to take the action. After about thirty minutes of going around and around, with most of the debate between two of the male partners, I asked, "Why don't we stop the discussion, call the governing body that has requested that we take this action, and ask for clarification of what happens if we don't do what we have been asked to do?" An African American female and an African American male partner agreed, but an Anglo partner continued to push the debate on this issue. After several more minutes of ranting and raving about why he thought we shouldn't do what had been requested of us, he couldn't get anyone to agree with him. He then said, "I suggest that we call the governing body that has requested that we take this action and ask for clarification." At that point, I interrupted him and asked if he was repeating what I'd said thirty minutes earlier, if he was trying to claim credit for my idea, or if he thought it was his. I also reminded him that he uses this tactic often and that I took it as a dismissal of my idea until he could try to claim it as his own.

On a number of occasions, I have been involved in detailed discussions about important topics, and the groups have taken a bit of time to explore ideas and options. When I spoke up about my thoughts, the leader would dismiss me by saying something like, "Let's not get into all that detail, it's time to move on." It's not likely that, as the CEO of your institution, you will experience this from a subordinate, but it's necessary for a woman CEO to present her ideas in a clear, precise manner so that no one in the room misinterprets where she stands.

✠ Tested

Women leaders in Annis' gender awareness workshops said it was not unusual for a male subordinate to be mistaken for the leader in situations where job titles and positions were unknown, and that they were often tested to see what their skill levels were. Perhaps some of this is caused by the male subordinate, who doesn't seem to notice what's happening, or more importantly, allows it to happen in certain settings.

I once took my leadership team to lunch at a private club and, while it was known that my assistant had made the reservation in my name, the server still asked who was to receive the bill. I told him I would take it. When he brought the ticket, he gave it to one of my male employees who also happens to have a membership at the club. The server was embarrassed when I reminded him that I would take the ticket, and he responded by saying, "I thought it was okay to give it to John." I responded by saying, "It's my reservation," to which John replied, "I was just trying to help." This particular staff member had done other things that I thought were designed to test me, but herein lies one of the problems: Women encounter so many things that are annoying and to which men tend not to be subjected that we may sometimes overreact. I try to avoid doing so, but I'm probably guilty of falling into that trap from time to time. This leads to the next topic examined by Annis and Associates: "third sex."

�֎ Third Sex

Just as I have questioned the way I handled the bill at the club, women often second-guess themselves and try to make sure they're not viewed as the awful people they're sometimes accused of being. We, therefore, might find ourselves changing styles to try and match those of men, who don't get dismissed or tested as often. We don't want to be seen as the mad alligator, always snapping at someone. Young women, especially, are aware that they must conform, to a certain extent, if they are interested in moving up the ladder.

✖ Excluded

This is perhaps one of the most annoying complaints women have. It is so easy for men to exclude women from their "normal" activities. I had a boss who consistently invited my male colleagues to take planned trips with him. He assumed that the women on the team would have no interest in his trips, so he didn't invite us. He never gave an explanation for this, but he and the male colleagues would talk very freely among us about their three- or four-day outings. In these settings, we were excluded and dismissed.

✖ Disrespected

I have experienced disrespect throughout my career and have heard many other women mention this behavior. Just recently, one of my employees told me that she spoke to one of her colleagues about the way the colleague's assistant addressed her. She has no concern about being called by her first name, but she noticed that when she went to her colleague's office, his assistant would say, "Dr. Doe, Sue is here to see you." Sue also has a doctorate degree, but the female assistant would never acknowledge her as "Dr. Sue." When I was a vice chancellor one of my direct subordinates always referred to me by my first name. He never asked me if it was acceptable, and, actually, I didn't mind – until I noticed that he always referred to the men around him by their titles and last names. So one day I asked him why he called me by my first name, but called none of the others by theirs. He was very embarrassed, apologized and acted as though he hadn't noticed that he was doing this. Interestingly, this was also an African American male.

My experiences don't show a major difference between how African American women and other women are treated in this respect. I know of a white college board president who wasn't invited to a high-level meeting with old-guard businessmen because they wanted her college to let them use space on one of the campuses. Instead, they invited the male vice president, who is also Anglo. It would be interesting to know why they thought the woman president could be left out of such an important decision.

Connie Glaser is a guru of gender talk. She has written six books about gender communication. She doesn't try to make women feel good about themselves. Instead, she edges women on by reminding them of the disqualifiers they often place on themselves when speaking: "This might be a stupid question. . ." "I'm not really versed about this. . ." or "You might already know this. . ." She says women tend to apologize much more frequently than men do, and that women use the apology more as a ritual than as deliberate communication. Men look at an apology in terms of hierarchy: If you apologize, you submit.

✠ Summary

In the face of cultural norms and research studies, one has to know that women in leadership roles at all levels in the workplace are likely to be seen as the bitch. Since the CEO is thought to have the ultimate power in the organization, it should not come as a surprise that the CEO may be seen as the real bitch. So one of the questions to be asked of us, especially African American women, is how do we help to control the environments in which we work? When women take a power-yielding position about basic things like respect and dismissive behavior without addressing them, they leave themselves and others subject to continuation of such actions. When they speak up about how they're treated, they are not normally thought of as lady-like. So when I'm asked the question, "Can you lead like a lady and be respected like a man?" my answer is likely to be: absolutely not! Women inclined to be overly concerned about how they are viewed by those under their supervision are likely to waste valuable time and energy worrying about things that may never change, and if they do, they are likely to change very slowly.

The "chocolate truth" about leading like a lady and being respected like a man has not been fully told until you are reminded, if need be, that the "chocolate" in us adds another dimension to the story. Even with our current president of the United States being African American, many Americans still think race matters when it comes to ability and that the more chocolate one is, the less the ability. That thought is not lost within the country's established institutions. In the mid-eighties when I received my first promotion to a position of influence at my college, one of my white female colleagues was so distraught over my appointment that she felt the need to ask if I didn't think my job should've gone to a white woman. She went on to tell me that there were significantly more whites at the college than there were blacks, and that it was only right that the first major appointment of a woman should have gone to a white woman.

Discussions around this thought have been prevalent throughout my career, and since I have had several significant promotions, I have had to deal with that mindset for years. The fact that I am now the CEO doesn't mean that much has changed when people approach promotions on the basis of entitlement rather than who is the best fit for a position. The board of trustees gave employees at my college an opportunity to tell them what characteristics and skills they would like to see in their CEO. Some of those who responded, thinking that perhaps I would be selected, did not talk about the characteristics and skills they felt the CEO should possess; they talked about what they thought were deficiencies in my qualifications and why I shouldn't be the next CEO. Some actually said they thought the board should choose someone of a different ethnicity!

It is my belief that anytime a woman, especially a black one, is selected for a high-level position, particularly CEO, the board isn't looking for someone who knows how to act like a lady. Boards choose a person who they think can get the job done. I think the board that selected me did so because they thought I was tough enough to take care of the things they thought needed to be addressed. They knew the challenges would be great, and I don't think they were concerned about whether I could lead like a lady and be respected like a man. I think they knew that I could lead and they also thought I would have enough sense to do so with dignity.

5

LEADING AS AN AFRICAN AMERICAN WOMAN

My professional journey has allowed me to spend 32 years in higher education and more than three- quarters of this time in community colleges. I've committed to this sector because of a strong belief in their mission of open access, opportunity, and success for all who dare to move forward in their educational journeys and improve life for themselves and their families— regardless of age, race, gender, and preparation. I have found that the community colleges' willingness to embrace creativity, ingenuity, collaboration, and teamwork puts them at the cutting edge of higher education. However, I would be remiss if I did not acknowledge that who I am as an African American and a woman is central to what I do. Anything that I have achieved relative to anyone's definition of success is based on those two characteristics. Along the way I have overcome obstacles and accepted challenges. I've been lucky to work in tandem with individuals who simultaneously understand the bigger picture while recognizing the importance of details in accomplishing goals.

It's amazing that I began my career in 1980 as the first African American female to be hired as an admissions and financial aid officer at a well-known four-year college in western Pennsylvania, and I end it in 2007 as the first African American and first female hired to lead this community college. I have been and continue to be aware that my career is a compilation of the most challenging and rewarding experiences I've ever undertaken.

Through my various positions in admissions, financial aid, minority affairs, affirmative action, student life, adjunct teaching, and senior administration I have expressed my passion for student success. With the advantage of working within the community, I can meet the needs of the community as well as develop the next generation of dynamic leaders. I'm able to fulfill a role that remains unconventional for women, even in the relatively female-friendly community college sector. I've been exposed to behaviors and sentiments that I've fought to either emulate or erase since my entry into higher education more than three decades ago.

✠ Journey to Leadership

My journey to the presidency began in the small town where I grew up in a large family. As the second of nine children, I had no choice but to accept leadership at an early age. The oldest girl in the family, I paved the way for three sisters through academic success in high school and dating, although this latter activity, as my father would have it, was executed very sparingly. My oldest brother and I were expected to take care of the younger siblings, including four more brothers. We set the example even when we did not want to, because it was exceedingly important for us to be at the top of the class. While I didn't realize it at the time, we were being groomed to realize the dreams of our parents. My father wanted to be an architect but ended up in vocational school and carpentry classes even though he had an outstanding ability for mathematics and an affinity for designing and building projects. To this day, we still marvel at the very first bookcase he built that still stands in the family room. My mother didn't finish high school but was so committed to doing so, that after having nine children, she went back to night school and achieved her dream by finishing first in her class when she received her GED. Like many in my generation, there was an expectation of academic and professional success, and no one gave or accepted excuses for it.

My path to academic leadership was an unconventional one. I was the second in my family to attend college. In the 1970's, many people of color were integrating into majority colleges and universities for the first time; approximately 200 of my peers and I were no different in 1972. What we endured that first year was surreal: we had to create an escort service because we were unable to walk alone or be out at night due to the racial slurs and physical violence; we were told by majority faculty that we were not qualified to be in the classroom and had been admitted to fill a quota system or because of a special program instituted at the state level. During one incident, all twelve Black girls in a 500-women dormitory faced suspension due to a one-on-one physical altercation when a classmate had been called the "nigger" one too many times.

I completed that first year and the following summer, moved to New York City where I worked for the telephone company as a benefits clerk and a bank as a communications technician. Five years later, I returned to the same college to complete my education, having been told that with only one year of college, I could not be promoted to a job I had already mastered.

After having been denied a promotion in October, I returned to college to study secondary education with a concentration in English the following January. At that time, my dream was simple. Like many of my aunts who lived in the South, I focused on becoming a high school teacher. I loved reading, and I loved the language of English — creating sentences using the proper nouns, subjects, verbs, direct and indirect objects, participles, gerunds, infinitives, and complete thoughts. However, in 1980, I could not find a job in the small towns that dotted the Western Pennsylvania corridor. I could not understand it. I graduated magna cum laude, and I had recommendations from the best faculty members. Finally, someone had the courage to tell me that all was fine with my credentials; it was when I actually went in for the face-to-face interview that a problem arose. Not one of those small school districts had the guts to be the first to hire a black woman.

After a few months of trying to get work anywhere, I saw a job announcement for the local university. They were seeking someone to join the admissions and financial aid team, with a bachelor's degree and good verbal and writing skills. Based on my experience and my success in that environment, it was not long before I was asked by a professional colleague to join her and serve in the admissions office at a community college.

I can't say exactly when the idea of being a college president became real to me. I do know that I always wanted my boss's job, as I often found that she or he delegated a lot of work to me, work that was not always directly or even indirectly related to the functional responsibilities I had. I was always volunteering to sit on a committee or lead an effort when there were institutional issues we were attempting to overcome or student issues we were trying to solve. Even with my commitment, promotions did not come easy.

Initially, I worked in a system where if one was asked to serve in an interim position the next step had always been, if the performance was acceptable, to be appointed. At my first community college, I was asked to move into a director's position after the director was given a special assignment. We all know what special assignment in higher education is akin to — you have six months to a year to look for employment somewhere else. I served in that role for two years without a pay increase, just a stipend, and was looking forward to my permanent promotion and additional compensation After all, I knew and it was continually affirmed by all — most importantly, the campus President — that I had done an outstanding job. Enrollment was up by more than 10 percent, staff was working as a team, new procedures and processes were tried and proven to be successful, and the department was a model for others at the college.

Unfortunately, for the second time in my life, I realized that things are not always fair. To say I was confused, hurt, and angry does not even begin to describe my emotions. I had stepped in the shoes of a white male and performed admirably; my bosses were two black females at the associate dean and dean levels whom I considered mentors; and I had done all I was expected to do and more with no real additional compensation. Some of my colleagues were encouraging me to file a complaint with Human Resources and/or EEOC, while others just commiserated with me.

I conferred with my husband, my parents, and mentors and devised a different plan. I quietly began searching and interviewing for employment outside of that system. I did not want to be in a place where my work was not acknowledged and there was a culture of gender bias. Within 30 days, I had secured a position as Associate Dean of Enrollment at a four-year university. As I prepared to leave, I believed I owed it to the campus president to thank him sincerely for his support. As an African American male who led with character, commitment, and courage, I wanted him to know how much I appreciated his willingness to give me a chance to serve him in an interim capacity. I also knew that it was not easy for him as the first male of color in such a senior position within that system. Needless to say, he was shocked to learn that I was leaving; he believed that I was going to be appointed to the director's position. After asking me to give him a few minutes to make some phone calls, I was called to my boss's office and while I was offered the position, I was also told that it was audacious of me to think that with only a bachelor's degree, I could lead one of the most important departments in student services. The lack of a master's degree had not come up as an issue or item of discussion during the previous two years.

Due to the support of that President, I accepted the Directorship, turned down the Associate Dean offer, and enrolled in graduate school fulltime, taking evening courses. The lack of the proper academic credential would never be an unknown stumbling block for me again. I completed both the master's and doctorate in five years. I also learned to pay attention to who had my best interests at heart and who didn't. I asked more questions and sought advice concerning my own career development. I learned how to accept constructive criticism and use it to focus on continuous improvement. It became clear to me that no woman is an island. I realized that movement up the ladder of career success depended just as much on relationships as it did on being able to perform.

I also began to understand the need to speak up and speak out about injustices being committed on professional colleagues of color and on students of color. At that community college, we convened the Black Caucus, and I served as the convener for five years. During that time, there was more hiring, promoting, and faculty receiving tenure than at any time before for people who looked like me. Services and programs were added that focused on the needs of students and of poor communities having access to higher education. Even in the 1980s and early 1990s, we understood the role of data and its power when combined with commitment and courage.

✖ Situations and Circumstances of Leadership

I also discovered that leading a small department differs significantly from leading a division and even more so from leading an entire unit, or a large urban college. As a leader, your decisions are constantly questioned, either overtly or covertly, and you'll have those defining moments when the rank and file needs to understand who the boss is. I have had those, too, and all of those moments were based on color or gender, not my ability to actually do the job.

The first occurred when I accepted a vice presidency at a college in the South. I discovered early on that while the search committee recommended, and the president selected me as the successful candidate, three of the four deans who would report to me did not share that feeling. As a matter of fact, they were hoping that the search would be unsuccessful and one of the current deans, who did not have the academic credential nor depth and breadth of experience, would be asked to serve. The dean of enrollment services was a particularly frustrating individual with whom to work, and he was the one who wanted and expected that he should have been named vice president. He had a reputation at the college for being outspoken, omnipotent, and less than a team player. However, his relationship with the president — my new boss — accounted for his continued employment. I attempted to strike a deal with him; I would not allow anyone to prejudice my working relationship and expectations, and he could consider this a new start. It worked well until I began to ask for plans, actions, and results based upon his functional and divisional responsibilities.

I clearly recall one grueling discussion when he indicated that he was not going to sit in my office, be subjected to a series of questions, and get into a "pissing contest." After about five seconds of mental shock, I knew this was the last disrespectful dialogue I was going to have with him, and I had to respond. So, I politely told him that, "pissing with him would never be a contest because

I could do it longer and further and he was never going to win." I asked him to leave the office, and that was the day I made the decision to remove him from student services and seek termination of his employment with the college. While I was eventually successful in removing him from student services, I had to be mindful of his extremely close relationship with the president. His termination was an item for discussion on my one-on-one agenda with the president every time we met for one year. I did everything the president asked me to do to re-direct the dean's work, and the dean hung himself. What he did not realize was that I, too, was building a relationship of fairness and trust with the president. Finally the day came when the president stepped aside and allowed me to do what had to be done. The lesson I learned with that dean is that patience and documentation are truly virtues.

Similarly, I recall, after being on the job for about one year, an employee filing a grievance alleging salary inequity and employment responsibilities that covered a 25-year period. Needless to say, none of this occurred on my watch. I was shocked and disappointed. Upon review of issues raised early in my career there, I had attempted, with the support and input of the staff, to make clear and distinct policies, rules, and procedures about the responsibility and division of work in the area. While the allegations proved unfounded, I subsequently discovered two things: that words and actions are not equal, and that sometimes employees of color have greater expectations of women or other persons of color. If that expectation does not come to fruition, they are more likely to seek redress. I learned to be thick-skinned and not to constantly question my own actions or decisions but rather to trust my ability to make decisions within the laws that exist and the policies that govern.

✳ Working in the Community College Sector

Why did I choose to nurture my leadership potential in the community college rather than in another setting? In only a short time at the community college, I saw what research confirmed: community colleges are the new model for higher education. Across the nation, community colleges have been springing up in urban, suburban, and rural locations; enrollments continue to grow; new programs are appearing; and young professionals are joining the faculty and staff. I got in on the ground floor of a burgeoning institution.

Community colleges offer an abundance of opportunities for leadership, particularly for women and minorities. According to the American Association of Community Colleges, 72 percent of community college CEOs are male, 81 percent are white, and 37 percent are between 55 and 59 years old (2009). With a large cohort of these CEOs expected to retire over the next several years, the community college sector presents great opportunities for leadership. At my institution, we are already realizing these opportunities. Women make up 57 percent of the senior team, 61 percent of all administrators, 60 percent of academic deans, and 60 percent of full-time faculty. Persons of color are 43 percent of the senior team, 63 percent of all administrators, 40 percent of academic deans, and 42 percent of full-time faculty.

Within the community college, I have found the flexibility to balance family and work life. When I joined the college as vice president for student services, my son, who is now a junior in college, was five years old and so I took advantage of the college's onsite kindergarten program. I am extremely fortunate to have a supportive network of colleagues and friends. When my husband unexpectedly passed away I was overwhelmed by the outpouring of sympathy, love, and support from the college and community. For me, community colleges have been extraordinarily welcoming and rewarding places to work.

Leadership That Makes a Difference

This supportive environment ensures more than my personal success. It ensures the success of my efforts to help students and the community reach their potential. Student success is one of our top institutional priorities, and I know that is shared by the 1,200 community and technical colleges nationally. We must continue to stand up and speak up for black, brown, red, and yellow students, many of whom do not have the academic prowess or the financial resources to take advantage of what higher education offers. When students are given opportunities to improve their individual quality of life, the impact on the communities in which we all live is tremendous.

Each year, I witness hundreds of students, many of whom would never have dreamed of higher education, walk across the stage during commencement. I take pride in their accomplishment, and I realize how humbling it is to know that in some small way, I have had a positive impact on their success. What I must do is what others have done for me: provide encouragement, resources, a listening ear, or a helping hand.

In addition to supporting student success, I fiercely believe that supporting communities is a cornerstone of college leadership. It is virtually impossible to extend oneself to the community without first learning about that community, identifying critical needs, and developing programs or services to meet those needs. In my community, I have gathered this knowledge as a member of the local school board and now as vice president of the state board of education in a variety of ways: serving on committees and boards, choosing a church home, and participating in community activities. I've found that community colleges are uniquely equipped to respond quickly to local and regional issues through initiatives and services focused on improving the quality of education, and subsequently, the quality of life for the residents it serves. But community colleges should give back outside of the classroom, too, so community service is also an institutional priority. Employees are encouraged to participate in activities such as volunteering in a hospital or food bank, raising dollars and awareness for local health or economic issues, helping to build a house, donating time and energy to work with voter registration or planning and organizing community events. I want my colleagues to join me in speaking out for those who are unable to speak for themselves and to donate time and money to help those in need.

⌘ Looking toward the Future

In these times of economic constraint, we face major challenges to our mission of providing access to education for our students, including the many women who enter higher education through the community college. As institutional costs continue to rise, I have struggled with whether to increase tuition when I know that our students are struggling too. While state and county governments have implemented layoffs and furloughs, we have avoided such extreme measures for now. Still, the college continues to grow in student enrollment and in programs. Our ability to accommodate this growth will surely affect our capacity to serve our students, including students of color and women who find opportunity in our classrooms.

My work as a senior administrator includes shaping and defining a vision, inspiring people to make that vision real, and helping them secure the tools they need to make real our goals and aspirations. I have found that leadership is not about the position; we are all leaders in some way. I have also discovered that the presidency does not define me; I define it. I have discovered particularly salient opportunities to define the presidency in the community college setting where I have been able to develop and implement new ideas, take risks, and pursue concrete opportunities for upward mobility. Discovering and nurturing my leadership potential has served me well throughout my educational, career, and life endeavors.

I also took, at every occasion, the opportunity to define what leadership meant to me. I studied the theory of leadership and learned from the doing of leadership. I have worked for at least five persons directly, about 15 indirectly, and four presidents. From each of them, I learned things that guided how I choose to lead. I moved up through the ranks, and I discovered that contrary to my early impressions, most bosses actually do work. Their work is just different from that of their subordinates. Most importantly, to me, however, is that in all of these 32 years of professional work in higher education, I have been most guided by what my parents and the elders in my community taught me. At a young age I learned to do unto others as you would have them do unto you, to remember that please and thank you are the most appreciated words in the English language, to walk with integrity, to appreciate the people on the way up the ladder because you may meet them on the way down, not to burn bridges, to never say never because you just might be confronted with that thing one day, to listen and learn, to do my best and lead by example knowing that nothing is beneath me and all is before me, and lastly, to lead with humility because at the beginning of the day, I put my nylons on one leg at a time like everyone else, and at the end, I pray to make the right decisions for the right reasons all the time.

6

A WOMAN'S WORK: MANAGING THE PROFESSION AND TAKING CARE OF FAMILY

All of us at some point in time have gained learning that serves us well for life experiences, whether shared with us by mentors, discovered through educational endeavors, or personally gained through trial and error. On moving from a dean's position to a vice president's position in a community college setting, I determined that I wanted to be sure to have time for my career, devotional and prayer life, family, and friends. To develop a strategy that allowed this, I interviewed women who I admired, and who were serving at the CEO level in various fields. I gained valuable words of wisdom that have served as principles to guide me as a career woman, wife, mother, daughter, and friend.

While there are many principles that I could share, I have decided to discuss those that have remained constant and have guided me for more than fifteen years. All of these life-sustaining guidelines have let me connect to the true essence of who I am, and have assisted me in developing a balanced lifestyle. Moreover, the principles all stress the importance of making time for what's important to me.

Principle 1: Learn to give away things that add no value to your life

One of the things that most impacted me was the integration of this principle into my approach. One CEO that I know sacrificed housework. She hired and managed the individuals that cleaned her home and kept her lawn. The value of time gained from having someone handle regular chores, like washing and folding clothes, created opportunities to focus on more important matters.

✠ Principle 2: Better organize time to devote to things you enjoy

I used to spend six to eight hours every week cooking. During those days, I spent time nearly every day preparing food, which I enjoyed, so I decided to re-arrange my cooking time for the week and devote it to Sundays after early morning worship service. Now, from 10 a.m. to noon, I cook several meats, vegetables and starches, and make one or two fruit salads. Some Sundays I also bake a dessert. Additionally, I strive to prepare some foods that I am able to freeze. With these foods in the refrigerator, my family has various options that allow us to customize our dinner meals during the week. When preparing family barbecues, large portions of meat are grilled so that half of the food can be frozen. This lifestyle change has let me preserve my special time in the kitchen while gaining four to six hours a week for other important matters.

✠ Principle 3: Prioritize according to your values

With more time in my schedule, due to having given up some things and better organizing others, I defined my top three values and identified areas for continued growth. The values that are most important to me are: 1) daily time for devotion and prayer; 2) weekly and/or daily time for relaxation and reflection; and 3) spending quality time with my son, mother, husband, and friends. I exercise these values in the following ways:

Devotional time – In reflecting on how to spend time daily with the Ruler of my life, I decided to begin my day with scripture, prayer and devotion. With this in mind, I rise each day, Monday through Friday at 6:30 a.m. and spend approximately fifteen to twenty minutes with scripture and music, and then about ten minutes in meditation and prayer. A bonus that I did not expect from this daily devotional time is that I experience an inner peace that allows me to have more peaceful days and creates more harmonious and relaxed mornings for my family. Regardless of what is going on, on the days when I include devotional time, I am less stressed.

Over the years, I discovered a variety of music, books, and devotional materials that I have integrated into this time. Later, I learned to follow this special time with thirty to forty-five minutes of exercise while continuing to listen to music and other spiritual materials on tape and/or television. I have added several exercise machines and appropriate technology to an area of my home. Recently, after being diagnosed as pre-diabetic, I learned that losing twenty-five to thirty-five pounds would significantly improve my health. I have since extended my special devotional exercise time, started eating healthier, and lost weight.

Personal time for rest and relaxation – When I was a teenager I had a routine of taking an hour-and-a-half to two-hour nap each Sunday. As I got older and became a working mother, I gave up this rest time. Now I have decided to return to the practice that gave me more energy. I start the week feeling rested and relaxed, more ready for work and better prepared for those unexpected situations that come with daily living. While this Sunday nap appears to be a small thing, it makes a big difference for me. Many of my friends know about this ritual. While some of them laugh, my best friends, mother, son, and husband respect my need for this extra rest. They don't bother me on Sundays between 3 and 5 p.m.

Quality time with loved ones – I truly love spending time in conversation and fun activities with people close to me, especially my son and husband, my mother, and my best friends. Over the years, I've learned to schedule dates for spending time with my loved ones at the beginning of the year. I try to confirm these get-togethers, at minimum, six months in advance. Of course, it's not the only way that I make time for those I love, but I place these important dates on my calendar so they become an important part of my schedule.

I have a wonderful mother who I love. I value the time that I spend with her. This relationship, like others, continues because of the time devoted to it. When scheduling time in advance, I look for opportunities to utilize institutional holidays, such as the Fourth of July. To ensure that I have the appropriate time to care for my mother as she becomes older, I save vacation time that may be used to look after her.

In examining areas for continued growth, I've learned to integrate topics into the various activities and discussions that I have with family and friends. In the last seven to ten years, I have organized a women's group that meets three days out of the year to relax and focus on an important subject that we identify in advance. Presently, we are focused on the topic of planning for retirement. Previously, we focused on defining and moving on to our next career change. We also spend time examining how each person may assist the others in the group. For example, improvement in the area of technology is something that I have to work on constantly. In addition to taking various professional development courses, I ask my best friends and son for assistance. Integrating learning with my conversations and interactions further allows for balance in my life in ways that are critical. Moreover, those in my life have shared that these scheduled activities make them feel valued and appreciated.

✠ Principle 4: Know your biggest role

One of the most cherished roles for me is that of being a mother. With my husband of more than thirty years, I have one son who we love dearly. Working to ensure that I have time for the role of mother is very important. All the roles I have taken over the course of my life have provided me with a sense of challenge, satisfaction, love and joy, and the principles I learned through these experiences are invaluable, but being a mom has given me more opportunities to learn and share wisdom. When my son was a baby, I invested in having someone come to my home each day to take care of him when I left for work. While it took me several attempts to find someone that I trusted, I finally hired a retired woman who became a valuable extended family member and kept my son for several years. This not only gave me peace of mind in knowing that my child was safe, it also gave me time each morning to prepare adequately with less rushing out to work. This resulted in a more relaxed environment for our family. Also, having a retired woman who had been successful in child rearing gave me a wise, experienced person to advise me on a number of matters.

Once my son started school, communicating with area churches that recommended childcare possibilities after class resulted in our securing another wonderful woman as his caregiver for more than seven years. She loved being at home with my son. She would not only pick him up from school, but she also transported him to baseball practice, community events, and various church activities. This caregiver was a good fit for our family because we shared the same core values and she also had the energy and desire to keep up with a teenager. As he got older, the caregiver would wait for him to come home rather than picking him up, so he didn't have to be teased about still needing a babysitter. This important change allowed my son to have a sense of independence after school while providing my husband and me peace of mind during work hours.

During my son's junior year in high school, after the death of our caregiver, our family selected a young pre-med student at a nearby university to provide my son with academic and mentoring services. This decision was made because we learned that the percentage of African American males completing high school was declining. In studying this matter, I recalled a wise woman suggesting that, during the teenage years, it became very important for young African American males to have someone near their age to mentor them. This young, African American male mentor was in our home two or three afternoons a week. We paid him a small salary that assisted him with his college costs, and he established a relationship with our son that helped our son learn more about the experience that college could be. With his academic background, this mentor was able to assist my son with math and science skills. I will never forget that my son was somewhat skeptical about having a college student visit with him. He thought he was old enough to stay at home alone. The very first day the college student came, he went to the computer and taught my son how to use some of the new technology to listen to music. This music activity won my son over, and he learned to look forward to the evenings with his mentor.

For as long as I can remember, I took my son to school a minimum of three to five days each week. Even when I had help picking him up, I always took him to class in the morning. I used this time for discussions about what was occurring in his life. I had some very special conversations with him and learned what was important to him. I recall conversations about a wide variety of such things as boy-girl relationships and knowing when God is speaking to you. As a family, we also spent time every Sunday having discussions about our values, problems and concerns. Sunday was the one day of the week that we worked to see that our entire family had a meal together. During his teenage years, I also had deep, meaningful discussions with my son before bedtime. One of the things that I had worked to develop with my son was a relationship where he felt comfortable talking to his parents about his problems and concerns.

One of the women CEOs that I interviewed had three children and shared how she made time for each child by selecting a sport to play with each one. She asked the child what sport they preferred. So when my son turned twelve I asked him to take racquetball lessons so that we would have additional time together. He liked this idea and we played racquetball at least once a week. This sport not only allowed me to enjoy special time and conversation with my son, but it added to my exercise program. Today, even at age twenty-five, when my son comes to visit, we enjoy a game or two of racquetball. Important conversations continue to take place during this physical activity.

For me, time with God, family, and friends is critical to a sense of balance in my life. Including special caregivers and male mentors helped my family to develop important relationships. Today, I am so thankful to have had in my life powerful women as role models who've made a difference with their words of wisdom about how balancing work and home has its rewards.

❊ PART THREE

SURVIVAL 1

How Do You Know When It's Time to Go?

Knowing the Signs of Trouble

Leveraging the Expectations of Your Board

7

HOW DO YOU KNOW WHEN IT'S TIME TO GO?

I've heard colleagues say things like, "I never saw it coming," "There was no obvious indication," "I was blindsided." Frequently, we find that there are multiple signs that it's time to leave a job, but one has to recognize them. For example, "John B." was president of a 13,000-student college campus in the Southeast. He was the second minority – but the first African American male – president in the system. After six applications and four interviews, he secured the presidency within the same state system where he had spent fifteen years at two other colleges, serving in various positions. The school was an independent campus in a system of twenty-eight others. Governance was historically collegial among faculty, collective bargaining units, and administration. Students had seats on the board and the faculty senate.

John's reputation portrayed him as smart, politically astute, and well-versed, if not well-traveled. He was also known to privately remind minority faculty and staff that he was morally bound to uphold the standards of the black middle class. As president, he was on all the appropriate civic, corporate, and philanthropic boards, and was frequently sought after to speak at local and state chamber, corporate, and graduation ceremonial events. John was also known to be rather autocratic, but he believed that most of his subordinates easily got over a rejection or accepted a decision he'd made after receiving little or no input. Faculty was an inconvenient necessity to John and his cabinet, a mere mechanism formed to validate his ideas. Prior to his arrival, the faculty and collective bargaining units had enjoyed an open-door policy with the president. John resisted all but the most necessary meetings with these groups.

He had worked hard for this position and followed the traditional route of faculty member, division chair, and vice president, all the way to the presidency. His relationship with the board chair was golden, and he was cordial with even the most difficult board members. Any given day found him popping in on employees, gifting them with pearls of wisdom on how to better run their respective operations and sharing with them the most recent research in their respective fields. However, under a seemingly calm, almost serene, campus climate was a seething cauldron of contempt for John's management style, apparent lack of sensitivity for the traditions of the campus, and – perhaps more damning – his perceived lack of respect for shared governance.

John was enjoying the first year of his renewed contract and was preparing for a two-week hiatus abroad. He was looking forward to a break after a tough year with the state and county budget offices. The college was able to maintain a flat budget, but John had to cash in some political chips along the way, and John knew these chips might be called at any time. A very popular and well-connected former vice president at the college had just returned to the area after a successful tenure with a for-profit organization and had let it be known that he was open to working again at the college, perhaps in fundraising.

Consistent with what one might imagine after experiencing a Stealth Bomber attack, the strike came suddenly and without fanfare: A week before the end of fall semester, John learned that a letter had been sent to the board from the faculty senate, two of three collective bargaining units, and the administrative council declaring a vote of no confidence. The closing statement in the certified letter to the board chair read, "We simply can no longer work with him. He is arrogant, patronizing, and uncommitted to shared governance." The board chair was surprised, though not shocked. He had received several e-mails and phone calls complaining about John's imperial attitude and style, but he never imagined that the discontent would rise to this level. Once John got over the initial outrage of it all, he immediately began calling in representatives of the constituency groups that had signed the letter. Surprisingly, each group found reasons not to meet, or declined the invitation before semester break. The die had been cast, the gauntlet tossed, and it was time to "get it on."

The human tendency is to do one of two things when threatened: fight or flee. The medulla reacts to a potent mixture of chemicals in the brain that can induce irrational behavior and/or extraordinary bravery. John experienced a bit of both. Not since his boyhood days in Brooklyn had he felt what he was emoting during this crisis. During high school, there had been some major challenges with bullies, gang members, and people who just genuinely disliked him and/or who were envious of his good grades and good-looking girlfriend. However, nothing in his professional career had prepared him for the news of that letter.

"How do you know when it's time to go?"

John pondered his options. He personally knew of several colleagues who had weathered votes of no confidence and had come to view them as badges of courage. After all, who was in charge, the faculty and staff or the president? The board had appointed John and he was going to lead, regardless of what the faculty and staff thought. John had carefully crafted on-campus alliances and made certain that he wasn't perceived as only the minority champion. Interestingly enough, the College's Equity Council hadn't come to his rescue; at least, not yet. The letter from the faculty and staff demanded action by mid-January. John had a week to ten days to make a decision in consultation with the board chair. His presidency was only in its fortieth month, and John was not yet vested. The board was split and the majority of the campus community was at a loss as to why this was happening and why now, just before the Christmas break. Consultation with several mentors and outplacement counselors suggested that John would likely secure another position in six to nine months if he resigned and moved on quietly before the vote of no confidence became public knowledge. The board chair could negotiate a gag order preventing discussion of John's departure. The sticking point was how much of a settlement he could expect. His contract guaranteed a year's salary (assuming no misconduct or malfeasance), should it be voided, and there was the potential for a tenured faculty position. But John was still not absolutely certain that he would leave, particularly if he could keep the board chair's support.

How do you know when it's time to go, to fight or flee? John sought advice from his wife and closest friends, but he didn't want his siblings and parents to know. Major points of consideration included the level of comfort remaining in either the president's role or as a faculty member on the current campus versus licking his wounds and starting over with a clean slate at a new college. He imagined that the vote of no confidence would follow wherever he went and, occasionally, precede him. John was appalled at how vicious some faculty and staff members became within weeks, calling his home and office and publishing vitriolic messages on blogs. Soon after the first weekend in January, John decided to leave, but with conditions: He negotiated a nine-month salary extension with full benefits and an agreement with the college for a favorable reference letter in perpetuity.

John had joined the ranks of failed presidents, a growing cohort of individuals from every background imaginable, including ethnicity, race, gender, sexual orientation, political and religious preference. John soon realized, however, that, for persons of color, it typically took twice as long, if ever, to secure a comparable position.

Before long, John was dwelling on thoughts about racial prejudice and racial profiling at the professional level, which appear to be incontrovertible conditions for people of color. Given the American social order, many minorities are exposed to, and challenged by, often unspoken, but strongly held, beliefs that people of color are somehow just not as smart, as competent, or as well-suited for leadership posts as whites. This stereotype is frequently an additional barrier to people of color as some over-prepare for seeking administrative careers and others are altogether discouraged from even applying for executive-level positions. John attempted to equate the crippling effects of racism and self-doubt into the process that decided who was selected for executive-level posts. How long can a racial minority survive? Or was it that ethnicity, gender, and race were not issues and, therefore, a convenient excuse for his lack of success?

John struggled with these questions for months as he attempted to selectively apply for presidencies, chancellorships, and executive-level positions in higher education on the east coast. Eight months out, he was applying for almost any position, anywhere, with the word "executive" in the title and that paid $75,000 or more. Search after search ended with him as a finalist, but he was frequently sabotaged by calls from his old college faculty to the institution where he was applying. John was getting desperate and the salary extension was running out.

About the same time, the stress of his imminent financial crisis began to reveal cracks in his personal relationships. Wife, siblings, parents and friends pleaded with him to pursue the government, corporate, and non-profit sectors, but John believed that he was destined to be a president again and wanted another shot. He knew and had personal contact with presidents who had been fired multiple times and continued to secure other presidencies. Most of them happened to be white males in their early to mid-60s. John was 56 and had no prospects.

Throughout his career, John had frowned on participating in minority caucuses. Yet, he wondered why none of the minority chancellors or presidents had reached out to him or offered him a position. John had been too embarrassed and proud to attempt leveraging any of the corporate or civic contacts he made during his presidency. Finally, after almost two years, a divorce and bankruptcy, John accepted a position in the federal government. The position was a two-year temporary assignment with prospects of multiple extensions.

What might we learn from John's sojourn? Were there issues of competence versus style (behavior) that could have been remedied, or was it just bad fit? The notion of "fitting" is critical to success in many venues, but particularly in college presidencies and, perhaps the community college, specifically.

Various alternative scenarios might have played out. They can be characterized under several themes:

- *Assessing the campus climate*

John's investment in learning the culture of his campus and the importance of shared governance prior to assuming office would most likely have resulted in a significantly different and more positive outcome.

- *Studying and practicing servant leadership*

Appreciating the principles of support staff and faculty as a leader who seeks to advance his subordinates and colleagues before himself would have been an advantage to John.

- *Critical communications patterns*

Effectively communicating with all campus constituencies in a regular and transparent manner would have likely provided early warning signals of trouble.

- *Internal environmental scanning*

Having mechanisms and relationships in place to help stay informed about critical (or mushrooming into critical) issues would have informed the president of the need to make changes.

- *Finding the right fit*

The proper temperament in the right setting and campus climate are crucial factors in successful presidencies. John might have given more emphasis to the conditions and climate at his college during his initial research of the position.

- *Other tidbits*

Building appropriate coalitions and networking with key campus leaders in both formal and informal positions of influence is important, as is establishing relationships with key individuals and groups off campus. Just as important as building relationships is creating, planning, and – potentially – executing an exit strategy that includes appropriate contract-separation language. Developing adequate savings and emergency funds, according to the financial planner rule of saving twelve months' worth of salary, is also wise.

8

KNOWING THE SIGNS OF TROUBLE

According to Webster's, the definition of trouble is "the quality or state of being troubled: an instance of distress, annoyance, or perturbation." It's further defined as "a cause of disturbance, annoyance, or distress: as a public unrest or demonstration of dissatisfaction." Other writers and historians have defined trouble as being caught up, trapped, down and out, out of luck, having no hope for today and a cloudy outlook for tomorrow. The word itself has been used for centuries to describe negative or bad situations. It's written in the Bible, history books, movies, and the like. Given its common usage, the word trouble still seems to get human beings' attention faster than any force on earth. All over the world, people are in trouble in one way or another. And as the poets and songwriters remind us, if you haven't encountered trouble just yet, it's on the way.

If you're in trouble — as we all are sometimes — my question is, why don't you always know it? If you search every reference, and consult every scholar, you'll find a different answer from each source. Although it's difficult to define, trouble, in some shape or form, seems to be the key factor when black and minority leaders fall from college presidencies. While the exact reason may vary from situation to situation, there are common factors that exist in nearly every fall from presidency for a black or minority leader. One of those factors, and the one that I feel is the most important, is that as minorities in charge, we simply forget that we are not them. We are not white people.

Too often when, as a minority, you reach the presidency or become the top CEO, you're replacing a non-minority who in most cases has been at the institution for a long time. You may have worked under the direct supervision of the person you replace. You may have known that person on a personal level or had a close relationship with his or her family. Along the way to the top, you may have watched or knew of things that the past president did that didn't fit well with your understanding of the policies and procedures of the college. For reasons unknown to you, and especially when these acts were performed in the public's eye, you convinced yourself that they were acceptable. You allowed yourself to become involved in discussions, activities, and meetings that you knew — or should have known — would not be good for you when you reach the top. Yet, you participated with them, enjoyed the trips, spent the funds, and seconded the motions. After all, everything was done in public, so why worry? You thought that you were learning the tools of the trade, but you were on your way to getting in trouble, and you didn't see it coming. You didn't know that their tools did not fit your hands. You didn't know that the good old boy approach didn't apply to you. You didn't know the free lunches, tickets to the concerts, athletic events, and VIP socials were not available to you. You tricked yourself into believing that the rejections were just poor timing and things would eventually get better. It happened so much that some of you got used to it. Getting to the top was your only goal at that time, and getting in trouble or causing trouble was the last thing on your mind. What you didn't know then, but soon learned, was that the seed was not only planted, it was now growing.

⚜ Reality Check

Once you've reached the top, and after all the celebrations and fanfares are over, the reality check sets in. You'll have set a goal for yourself to elevate the institution to a higher level, much higher than the last president and those before him or her. You probably believe that you can do it better, smarter, and much faster than the past leaders because of your inside knowledge. You've already watched how your predecessor led and performed, communicated with the boards, and interacted with community leaders. You noted how they collaborated with politicians to generate big grants and funds for the institution, taking time to study the success stories of the college and the community. You're prepared to give the good speeches. With all of that ammunition, you're excited about getting started as the person in charge, but you're forgetting something. You're not your predecessor, because we don't look like them.

We don't talk, walk, or act like them. Your discussions about family and past experiences are different. Even when you display pictures of your folks, it's clear to all that things are different. While you probably knew that the staff would have to get used to your new minority face, you weren't prepared for the long faces you get every time someone passes by. We have to remind ourselves that we are not them.

The reality check never takes long to set in. No longer than the publishing of the evening paper or the six o'clock news, depending on which comes first. The mere thought of hearing your name on television as "the first Black president," or reading the question in the local community paper asking is the college ready for a minority CEO, adds fuel to the reality check. Although in many instances you pretend to overlook the obvious implications, the little knot in your stomach is starting to act up. Yet, you remember all of your professionalism and set out to do your very best. Remember what you do have: you already know board members, either by personal introductions or comments in the minutes of the board meetings. Although personal contacts and special insiders inform you of the who, what, when, and where of the college family, you still march on with an open mind and a strong determination. Smile in the faces of those whom you know voted against you, and compliment those whom you know made negative comments to others about you. We have to remind ourselves that we are not them.

✄ Trust

The reality check will be an ongoing process, so you'll have to find someone you trust. Is it the secretary who witnessed the goings and comings of the last five presidents, or is it the dean who served as your host during the first visit to the college? Would it be the trustee or the board member who asked the tough questions during the interview? Trying to identify that special someone or group to trust is not an easy task. Reflect on your past and identify people who helped you and offered good advice. Canvass the campus, looking for that particular person or group that allows you to be yourself. It shouldn't take long, a few days or so, to realize that the two or three employees whom you may have labeled as quiet and reserved have all the answers you need. Some of you will be successful in finding that right and valuable trusting encounter. For those of you who have difficulty finding trusting relationships, direct your attention to creating a campus where employees are encouraged to be loyal to the institution, show support and confidence in the administration, and display a bond of trust amongst one another. If you can't personally find that trusting situation, create a campus where trust is planted in the foundation. You'll get off to a good start if you display a friendly, open, and honest spirit when approaching students and employees. Make it a priority to approach each day with a positive attitude, to ensure that everyone on staff works with a sense of appreciation and gratitude.

✠ Fortitude

While preparing for the challenges and oppositions that confronted you in your new role as president, after dealing with a reality check and lack of trust, you may find yourself asking the question: "What have I gotten myself into?" Knowing that there is no turning back, and you couldn't even if you wanted too, focus on fortitude. To be successful, demonstrate determination, courage, and endurance that'll allow you to deal with every situation that comes your way. Your mental energy will have to endure long hours and your heart has to be strong enough to overshadow fear and danger. Your experiences have prepared you well for this journey, so don't spend a lot of time dwelling on the obstacles. You'll find that the reality check won't faze you. This trip will be like adding another chapter to your exciting history. Don't ever doubt that you have the qualifications to get the job, the experiences to do it well, and the vision and toughness to see it through. But know that you have to be twice as good, twice as fast, and twice as strong as the person you've replaced. You have to remind yourself that we are not them.

✠ Tough Decisions

As a new president you must make the tough choice of who will stay and who will go. How do you keep top administrators from defecting? How do you encourage employees to trust in your leadership? In order to be as open and fair as humanly possible, you'll have to rely totally on instinct and courage. Although employees may be discussing and even betting on who'll be fired, transferred, or demoted, keep everyone focused. Even though you'll make it clear to everyone that you don't have a hit list, no one will be convinced, especially the clerks and secretaries in the president's office. After spending long hours presenting, discussing, and sharing your goals and vision for the college, most of the employees will be still be waiting for a change in the organizational structure. As the days become weeks, and weeks become months, you'll begin to identify the enemies in your camp. In most cases, enemies are the deans, administrative assistants, and clerks who work with you every day. For various reasons unknown to you, they feel they're subject to termination because of their support for the last president. To overcome this sense of insecurity, many of them work hard to get close to the person at the top. Some of them try to be friendly and supportive, while others try to show leadership that is invaluable to the college. The commonality that they possess is a need to be included in the president's business. They want the president to seek their approval, informally or formally, before announcing a project or activity. In other words, they want you to feel close enough to them to share ideas and information that would normally be reserved for a select few. Not only would this relationship give them a heads- up on their peers, but also it would give them campus-wide power, regardless of their jobs or positions.

⊠ New Leadership

Being the new leader on campus isn't only a new chapter in the college's history. It's also a new way of life for students, faculty, staff, administrators, board members, community leaders, and friends of the college. Knowing all of this, you'll want to make sure that you quickly get things rolling while not stepping on any toes, especially those that you'll walk around every day. You have to answer several questions that will serve as your guide as you reveal your leadership style. How would a good president involve key employees in the governing process? How does the new leader get employees to do their jobs in an acceptable manner, not because they are paid, but simply because they want to? Should the president create a cabinet or appoint an administrative council? Should the president have an open door policy, or should everyone make appointments? Think about your answers, but you'll certainly need to make decisions, and the sooner the better. You may be the type of new CEO to struggle over these decisions, or maybe you know exactly what you want to do. All college presidents want a happy and loyal staff that will get their jobs done in a friendly and professional manner. However, deciding how to involve them in the business matters of the college is your major concern.

To ensure that you don't make the same mistakes as the past president, study and review their management style. You'll never hesitate when problems are presented, rather you'll handle them without delay. By implementing your skills and expertise, you can show all of your critics who might have had doubts that you're the right choice, that you can make tough decisions, and that the college is in good hands. What you may not realize right away is that some of the problems have long, complex histories that cannot be resolved in a short time. What you do not know at first is that some of the employees referenced in the past, as well as the ones referenced in current problems, had close relationships with college administrators, trustees, and board members. Some of them had high positions with few or no qualifications. Some of them simply had no work responsibilities. Some of them did absolutely nothing; they were just on the payroll. You might find that your staff is comprised mostly of consultants, rather than regular employees. Without hesitation, you may have started the evaluation process thinking that you could immediately correct the problems and assure all faculty that in the future every employee would earn their pay. On the other hand, you might have adopted the attitude "if it ain't broke, don't fix it." You thought that since employees had been on the payroll before you got there, and everyone knew it, why rock the boat? Regardless of what you decided to do, you know now that you have to prepare yourself for the war that is to follow reorganization. If you attempted to fix the problems or if you allowed them to continue as usual, either way the war is near.

As you go about your daily routine, you'll start to notice that the atmosphere of cooperation, love, and support that initially flooded your office is diminishing little by little. You may be puzzled by this drastic and unexpected change, or understand exactly what's happening and why. At this time, you need the support of the employees, community leaders, trustees, and board members, but you also have to make some decisions that would probably cause them to become angry and upset. As you now reflect on the encouraging remarks made by the chairman of the board when you were hired and the charges given to us by community and civic leaders urging us to put the college house in order, you cannot help but wonder if those words will carry you through this crisis. It may feel like taking a long trip with only a few known destinations. Your map shows either success cities or failure states. Even your navigators are limited to scenic or quickest. The then and the now are certainly two realities with two different purposes. It was quickly becoming the —best of times and the worst of times."

✠ Get Ready, 'Cause Here We Come

The next three to five months are key — you'll need to make the personnel changes in a short time span. Cut spending, reduce travel, develop a new mission statement, restructure the foundation, reorganize your cabinet, add new members to the college advisory council, join the local chamber, and visit all the college trustees. In spite of all of your efforts to establish a positive and professional approach though, things may begin to feel a little different. Those employees who worked hard to get close to you may start to pull away. The invitations to social and community events come to a complete halt. Even the janitors, who always provided you with kind words of wisdom, look at you a little differently or don't even look at all. You know something's happening, and you certainly don't feel good about it. And even after looking over the changes that you made, you still can't understand what's happening. No matter what you do to provide the best leadership possible, you're questioned and/or second-guessed by nearly everyone at the college and in the community. You'll start to think about your future at the college and what steps you need to take to ensure that you don't wait until the walls cave in, you're terminated, or asked to resign.

After a short period of searching and searching, trying to make sense of this overnight transformation from being the leader of choice to the CEO without a face, you'll recognize the calm before the storm. You may choose to prepare yourself for whatever comes your way, or fool yourself that a change will come. You'll be forced to take a good look at your situation: you're in trouble. Pull out the old job announcements and day by day, silently search the job markets to find that perfect match. Keep your head erect, your attitude positively adjusted, your heart full of love, and your tears carefully tucked away. You have to project an image that will convince all employees that you're still in control of the college and capable of making good decisions. Although it isn't easy to pretend everything's okay, it's something you have to do. As the pressure mounts from every side, your life starts to change. You may feel yourself becoming sick or weak, angry or out of control. In the past, some of us have gone to the bottle, while some went to prayer. Regardless of the methods we've all used to deal with our problems, we had trouble trying to find a quick resolution to what had become our professional mess.

✠ What's Next?

As a minority president fallen from power, you may be lucky enough to find another job without delay, while a large number of you find the pathways blocked by political enemies, resentful past employees, and individuals and groups that don't think the college is ready for a person of color. For those of you who will have difficulty securing new jobs, use your time off making contact with friends across the United States and in other countries. Let them know of your search and that you're in need of help. Some of you, especially the ones who act like you've made it to the top all by yourself, won't want anyone to know that you're in trouble. You'll go about your daily routines; attending conferences, actively working on boards, running for the positions, and playing the big-shot roles without ever letting others see or sense your pain. And a few of you will be able to hold out without anyone ever knowing the troubles that you've experienced or the roads you've had to travel to get back on your feet. Regardless of whether our roads to recovery are similar, we all have to deal with the fact that our status and roles as presidents of our respective institutions are fading. In the end, some of you will receive non-renewal letters, some phone calls, other will see visits from board member and trustees, and yes, some will get the message in the chat room. If that's not bad enough, some will hear the news of your firing or forced retirement in emails, while some will receive the announcement when you're watching the news on television.

It may take a while to accept the fact that you have to start a new journey. You'll struggle with how to tell family and what to say to friends, coworkers, and peers. For a period of time, you may not know what to do. For those of you who've stayed active with boards and commissions, you can put in the calls and make the visits. Those who've disassociated from the boards, committees, and commissions that had helped you to reach the top, will have nobody to contact. Some of you thought you no longer needed to associate with your fraternities, sororities, lodges, and other community and social groups. You completely disowned and alienated yourselves from the Presidents' Round Table and other diversity associations. Some of you thought that you'd made it, and stayed away from meetings and gatherings where there were a lot of us — people of color. However, after the fall, you have nowhere to go and so you go back home to share your sad stories and refuel your tank. As strange as it seems, you'll now understand the thoughts and feelings of the prodigal son when he went back home to his father after having spent all of his goods. And like his father, the Presidents' Round Table and a few of your old associations will welcome you back with open arms. Regardless of the situations and/or circumstances, the majority of you will know how to find your way home. You may just have to be forced or encouraged to go back and face the family. You're not really caught off guard when you're met with smiles, big hugs and kisses, and all those kind words of love and encouragement. After all, you know that family doesn't change. Although it's hard to accept, you know that you were the ones who had experienced temporary memory loss. Nevertheless, you're back and very happy to be among family and friends.

At the end of the day, you have to analyze the situation, suck it up, and move on. You'll try hard to identify and define your problems. Deep inside all of us, we all want to know why we were so blind and didn't see the signs. You'll review your leadership styles and management techniques; you went through a reality check, went through the steps a new leader should such as trust and fortitude; and you thought about the tough decisions you had to make. You thought about everything in hopes of finding the real reasons for your failure. Through it all, you need to face the realization that it's over, and pray for a better tomorrow.

We've all prayed as we prepare to leave, but I cannot forget the question that one of our brothers so clearly asked all of us: "If you are in trouble, why don't you know you are in trouble?" As strange as it may seem to some of us, the answer to this question is blowing in the minds of many of our world leaders. I thought the question had been answered when we sent a man of color to the moon, and we were all assured that our time had come when we had Black doctors and nurses in leadership positions. When some of our major colleges and universities accepted the fact that people of color could quarterback and call the plays on the court, we knew that the world had made a complete reversal and success could be ours if we only believed. And we all know that if the question of trouble is asked of our leader in the White House, what he would say to be politically correct and what he honestly feels would be worlds apart. All leaders, regardless of their titles and/or positions, should be grateful and thankful that our President of the United States of America has not forgotten that he is not them.

When my friend Earnest put before the Presidents' Round Table a profound and powerful question — "If you are in trouble, why don't you know you are in trouble?"— I said it then, and I say it loud and clear today, especially in today's troublesome and tea party atmosphere: As minorities, too many of us simply forget that we are not them.

9

LEVERAGING THE EXPECTATIONS OF YOUR BOARD

Once you've decided to become a community college chief executive officer (CEO), you then have to decide which type of structure fits you best. There are three options: you may be responsible for leading a college that is within a defined community or service area with a reporting relationship to a higher level CEO, typically a chancellor; you may be responsible for the daily operations of a college and report to a board; or you may join a multi-college or multi-campus system in which the CEO supervises college/campus presidents, has responsibility for the entire system, and reports to a board. Both of us decided early in our careers that we would never choose the third option. However, after years of reporting to a CEO, we both gained experience and yearned for greater challenges, which we found by moving into the logical next step of reporting directly to a board.

We've been friends and colleagues for 15 years and have a combined total of 30 years as CEO. We've had numerous conversations with each other and our peers about the myriad challenges we face. The following is one of our typical exchanges on the subject of working with boards. We share the opinion that the goal to become a CEO is one that is not easily made, but once fulfilled you're in for the job experience of a lifetime.

****

Ned: As a 17-year veteran CEO, I have come to learn that nothing is as easy as it looks. My first observation of a college president was as a 21-year-old recent college graduate who thought I knew everything. I saw a 60-plus-year-old president walk across the university campus and thought to myself, all he does is sign papers and go to meetings; I can do that.

Helen: My experience was quite the contrary, my friend. My first observation of a college CEO occurred when I was an undergraduate, involved in student government at a time when students were protesting against everything. I had many opportunities to observe our president as he responded to a variety of issues. I even served as a student trustee and participated in board meetings. That was when I became convinced —at 20 years of age — that there was no way I would want such a job.

Ned: I can see that you took that to heart.

Helen: And I can see you've learned that being a CEO is more than signing papers and going to meetings.

Ned: Most definitely. The enthusiasm and arrogance of youth is wasted on the young. Even now as a 60-year-old chancellor, I find myself in awe of those who make the job seem effortless. Working with a board of trustees or any governing board is one of those activities that, on the surface, seems easy, but the subtle interactions between the board and the CEO are only observed by the most careful onlookers.

Helen: I agree. I really enjoyed my CEO work at the college level, reporting to the district CEO and not the board. From observing my boss at the time, I could not imagine being away from the everyday business of a college and not having interactions with students, faculty, and staff on a daily basis. I was in the trenches, and could not imagine myself in a more corporate and rarified environment where I had to interface with board members and deal with the more political aspects of being a community college CEO. Reporting to a board would mean I would have to become more politically astute than I was at the time.

Ned: The political aspect of the job is the toughest. As a relatively new CEO about 15 years ago, I could not always distinguish between who was the nominal leader and who was the actual leader of a board. I also didn't understand that boards, like family members, stick together when actions of the total board are in question by an outside entity. It took me longer than a person of average intelligence to understand who really ran the state system of which I was a part.

Helen: It sounds as though you have an illustration to support this lesson.

Ned: Illustrations are often valuable teaching tools. I worked for a board that was created by gubernatorial appointment. The president of this board was a former legislator and was appointed to the board because he was a staunch supporter of the governor. As a new CEO, I actually thought that the board controlled policy for my college and other colleges in the state system. During a board meeting, I dutifully observed one of my colleagues follow the direction of the board president regarding a personnel decision effective June 30. My colleague asked to discontinue the contract of an administrator that would create a vacancy at the college effective July 1. I was present during the conversation when the board president granted approval without qualification for the discontinuance of the contract. Neither my colleague nor I knew that the administrator subject to discontinuance was a personal friend of the governor and that the governor had not granted prior approval for the dismissal of the administrator. Upon hearing of the dismissal, the governor terminated the CEO without process and then created a circumstance wherein the CEO was seen as incompetent. The CEO still has not been able to find employment as a CEO since the governor impacted his reputation. The governor, not the board president or the board, made this decision. The entire board supported the governor in terminating a CEO who had received board support just one day before his termination. Understanding who's actually in charge has an impact on the decision-making process in an environment. I learned that this board was important in administering the governor's decisions, but that the governor set policy, not the board.

Helen: The good part of that story is that you were an observer and not the main player. That's probably the best way to learn a lesson, from observation and not being a major player. I know from my current position that actually being in the seat is not at all like being an observer. I had been a fairly close observer of the interactions between the district CEO and the governing board for at least 10 years before becoming the district CEO, and so I thought I had anticipated everything. Was I wrong! I learned the hard way that there is nothing like being in the seat.

Ned: I know exactly what you mean. I am having a similar experience now myself. What did you discover to be the biggest difference in your perception of the job and the reality you faced once you were in the job?

Helen: Well, I knew reporting to five bosses would be challenging. However, the reality was much more difficult to face than I had originally thought. I am thankful these days that there are only five members; I cannot imagine how CEOs can keep up with more than five. Each has differences in personality; knowledge and experience of their role, the district, community colleges; causes; interests; and reasons for their service. I realized after my first board meeting that I needed to get myself organized and learn very quickly how to work effectively with the board. Learning that lesson would be the key to the success of the district.

Ned: So what did you do immediately?

Helen: In the first three months, I found myself a mentor, a seasoned CEO who had worked with boards successfully for a number of years. He was open to me, and I could call him at any time. Let me insert here that I did not make a nuisance of myself but felt comforted by the fact that he was there if I needed him. I also read current literature on board-CEO relationships and roles, and shared those readings with the board president. I spent a day with the longest-serving CEO in California to learn from her and ended that day by attending their board meeting. I also talked with my counterparts throughout the country to increase my knowledge and understanding of my new role. Perhaps the most important thing that happened in those first three months was a board retreat. The board had not had a retreat in at least eight years. The board members agreed that they needed an opportunity to bond as a group and to review their role and responsibilities as they began their work with a new chancellor. A facilitator, skilled in working with community college boards, was employed to guide the board through the retreat activities, which resulted in a more unified board with a clearer understanding of each other and their role. I've also learned a considerable amount about my role when it comes to working with the board. Knowing and adhering to the appropriate role is as important for the CEO as it is for board members.

Ned: Even now as an experienced CEO, I have to remind myself that the meeting of the board is not a meeting of the board directed by the CEO. While I know more about the day-to-day activities of the college district, I'm often challenged to remind myself not to substitute my opinion in place of the board's role in making policy. As CEO, I have strong positions on many subjects, yet the board is imbued with the public responsibility. As an example, the board was engaged in a long debate as to whether to fund a child development program. The board and general community differed in opinion concerning the effectiveness of the program. The community saw the program as a great public resource, while the district staff saw the program as a drain on district resources as well as an activity out of alignment with the mission of the district. Over a period of two years, the board held public hearings on topics such as funding and staffing alternatives for the program. It's important to note that board members were involved in re-election campaigns during this time and were careful not to bring undue attention to these debates. As CEO, I wanted to bring closure to this discussion, and I was sure that the question wasn't as complicated as the parties made it out to be. During an open meeting on the topic, I allowed my assuredness to enter the discussion. I was clearly, yet firmly, reminded that my role was different than that of an elected board member. I kept quiet from that point on; I had learned my lesson. The meetings are not structured so that the CEO can tell the board what it ought to do. Board meetings are just that: board meetings.

Helen: You've worked in four different positions in two states and participated in more CEO searches than I have. Have you ever walked away from an opportunity to report to a board?

Ned: As you know, I have a story on every topic. Working for a board doesn't always involve selecting from a set of rational choices. It does, however, involve a clear knowledge of your ethical boundaries. As a young prospective CEO, I was offered what I considered an unethical — some might even determine illegal — choice by board members in a community college district. This five-member board interviewed me and another finalist for the CEO assignment. Accordingly, one member was tasked to meet with me privately after the public interview. During the private conversation, the board member told me that I could count on support of two of the five board members. In order to get the third vote, the board expected $15,000 in reimbursement of board election expenses. I was informed that an "extra" $15,000 would be included in my base contract, but I was clearly expected to provide these funds directly to board members. I should have been suspicious to begin with as this conversation took place after hours in the restaurant of a casino card room.

Helen: Surely, you jest!

Ned: I do not. After this sobering conversation, I sought and received advice from an experienced CEO. The advice I received and heeded was to start running from this crazy board and never look back. Eventually, another CEO was hired. The new CEO had a relatively short tenure, and the board members in this district were eventually stripped of power. Some were indicted, convicted, and served prison sentences.

Helen: You wisely escaped a job that would have ended in disaster for you as it did for those trustees. That was probably some of the best advice that you've been given in your career. As a result of that experience, what advice would you give someone who is interviewing for a CEO position that reports to a board?

Ned: The CEO assignment has to be in alignment with your values. The work is difficult under the best circumstances. It becomes impossible if values and ethics are not aligned with the work.

Helen: I emphasize communication with the board as critical. This was another area I thought I had covered until reality set in. When I started as CEO, I would send a one-way communication to the board at least every two weeks to apprise them of activities of the district and information I thought to be important. I also met with the board president monthly to review the agenda for the upcoming board meeting. In my second year of tenure, the board agreed that the pre-review of the board agenda should be with the president and vice president. Including the vice-president in these meetings ensured that the board meetings would continue to run effectively under his or her leadership. To this day, I hold these meetings and consult with the president and vice president between meetings, regarding any policy matters that require board attention. Effective communication ensures the board fulfills its appropriate role and that I fulfill mine.

****

As in this exchange, we often talk about our work. For both of us, it is about our commitment to helping others and making a difference because of the sacrifices that so many have made for us. There is a great deal of satisfaction in the work and in always trying to leave things better than we found them.

PART FOUR

SURVIVAL 2

Life After a Vote of No Confidence

When Uncertainty Reigns

To be or not to be An inside Applicant, That Is the Question

10

LIFE AFTER A VOTE OF "NO CONFIDENCE"

I believe that the so-called no-vote is rarely related to the fulfillment of the president's job description or lack thereof. In my case, it was purely emotional and had nothing to do with my accomplishments. Whether the vote is just or not, it will follow you mentally and professionally. You'll find yourself wondering how it happened and what you could've done to avoid it. During job interviews, it'll be the dark cloud above your head. You would think, therefore, the no vote should be avoided at all costs. In my case, however, I continued on a path that in all probability was headed toward a vote of no confidence. I did it because it was what I believed in, and what I had to do.

The Problem

Troubles began when I refused to fire an administrator that the faculty senate president wanted terminated. I should mention that the administrator was my vice president for student affairs and a strong black male. The faculty senate president was a white female and felt that she had been slighted by the VP at a student event. The college was located in the heart of the South, with a non-unionized workforce. I hasten to add that the college culture reinforced a subtle but strong anti-feminist, southern belle social structure. The faculty senate president was respected by her mostly white colleagues. She appeared to be student-oriented, kind, and liberal. She viewed herself as part of the old Southern aristocracy.

The VP had done an excellent job in student affairs. He was a strong supporter of the college and was active in the community. He made things happen! He was a loud supporter of student activities and a strong student advocate. The students really liked him, and the student body was 80 to 90 percent African American while the faculty was 80 to 90 percent white.

✠ Setting

This was my first presidency. I was young, eager, and arrogant. The college was located in the hood. It was an urban, inner-city, comprehensive community college. The students were from the community and represented mostly African Americans from all walks of life. It's redundant to say that the students were from working-class backgrounds, because in the South most blacks have a strong work ethic and work either in factories, entrepreneurial occupations, or corporations. In addition, 70 to 80 percent of the students were on Federal financial aid. The college population had grown from 1,500 to 7,000 in little more than a year. The VP and I had engineered a plan to increase enrollment. The plan was working, and the college was growing. Some were excited, and others not so much. Some faculty complained about having too many students in their classes. Others were extremely happy to be teaching full classes as well as having the ability to teach overloads. There were approximately 80 to 90 full-time faculty members, approximately 70-80 percent of which were white. All the custodial and student services staff were African American. Approximately 70 percent of all other support staff was African American.

✠ The Data

African American faculty members were paid half as much as their white counterparts. It was incredible, but it was true in 1996. I discovered this fact one day when I was having a casual conversation with an African American faculty member. I asked him how long he'd been employed at the institution, and he proudly replied that he'd been there for 19 years. When I asked how much he earned, I was shocked to find out it was merely nineteen thousand dollars, after all that time. I tried hard not to let on to my incredulity. The conversation ended, but I was chagrined at the thought that a tenured, associate professor with stellar years of service would be at the low end of the salary schedule. My interest was piqued. I decided to order a copy of salaries for all faculty. I was surprised to find that the entire black faculty was at the low end of the salary scale. I had the list disaggregated by rank, years of service, and teaching discipline. African American faculty consistently were not only at the bottom of the salary scale but in all instances earned only half as much as their white counterparts.

I reported my findings immediately to the chancellor, who also was African American. We strategized to create a salary study and make appropriate salary corrections. Yet there was one little problem. We needed to improve enrollment in order to have enough funding to make salary increases happen. I had begun the job during spring semester. By the following spring, we had increased enrollment from about 1,500 students to approximately 7,000 students. Subsequently, as faculty observed and noted, classes were full, and they were teaching more.

They demanded an increase in salary, and the words were music to my ears. The plan was working. Student enrollment had finally increased enough, and we could afford a faculty increase. Of course, my harangue was the usual, "Equity and parity, blah blah blah." Not surprisingly, the white males were quaking in their boots. I requested the faculty senate to provide ten names from which I would select five for a salary increase committee. I selected a committee comprised of two white males, one white female, one black male, and one black female. Subsequently and collaboratively, we selected a research firm to provide an analysis of faculty salaries and to make appropriate recommendations. Everything went well. The research firm took about a month to do its work. The faculty committee members received the data and began their deliberations. They took another month. We were on schedule to complete the process and provide faculty raises by the fall.

Some of the deliberations began to leak out and became grist for debate at the faculty senate meetings. I agreed to attend a senate meeting and be questioned with respect to rumors that many African American faculty would be receiving increases while whites would not. One white faculty member said that I was creating a race war. Another said, "We love our colored faculty, but it is unfair that they should be paid more." I selected one example on which to hang my — or I should say — from which to be hanged. I selected an example using the faculty senate president and the same departmental colleague who had started me on my investigation. During the meeting, I asked, "Madam President, how long have you been employed at this institution?" She replied, "I have been employed for 19 years." "What is your rank?" I asked. She replied, "Associate professor and I have worked very hard to achieve this rank." I asked, "Do you believe that all associate professors ought to receive similar pay considering that promotion means that all who are promoted have earned it and deserve to be paid for it?" She replied, "I do." I asked, "Then, would you say that it's grievously unfair if any of your colleagues, who have been promoted to associate professor, were grossly underpaid?" She replied, "Yes, it would be very unfair." I proceeded to emphasize the values of unfairness and inequity. In my opinion, the problem of achieving salary equity was only part of the issue. The problem of achieving faculty equity for all was the real issue. A secondary issue was that these poorly paid faculty members, all African American, had been underpaid for years, maybe as long as a decade. Therefore, even if we solved the immediate problem, we could not undo the years of humiliation, degradation, and unfairness suffered by the long-term African American faculty. The white faculty suffered, too, and many who cared had grown blind and numb to the pangs of inequity and injustice. The institution suffered also. It did not have respect from its sister colleges.

✠ Victory

We pushed through the new salary schedule. It took nearly one year from its inception. We set up a rubric that allowed for those who had been underpaid to be paid according to their rank and their merit. I got the committee to agree that there would be salary ranges within which faculty would be placed according to their merit. For example, at that time, the range for an associate professor was $35,000 to $45,000 base salary per annum with adjustments for merit such as departmental evaluations, papers published, conferences attended, student evaluations, college service, and committee service. The protagonist of this story received an increase of at least $19,000. The entire African American faculty (20 to 30 members) saw their pay at least doubled. No white faculty member lost any pay, and all received something. As I recall, the slightest increase that a white faculty received was about $1,500. The faculty had not had an increase in a few years. As you might imagine, I was a hero to the African American faculty and a villain to the white faculty. I requested that those whites who were unhappy should refuse the pay increases, yet no one did.

✠ The Battle

Usually, the battle comes before the victory but not in this case. It was on! The fairness argument made no sense to the white faculty. The majority of all of the departments consisted of white faculty. By and large, white faculty had selected these African American faculty members in legitimate searches and had voted them to be tenured and appropriately promoted. Nonetheless, I could not convince the white faculty concerning fairness of pay equity for their African American colleagues.

During the next several months, every administrator was under close scrutiny by the faculty and under constant fire. Every administrative decision was criticized. Every administrative action was cast in a negative light. Even the increased student enrollment came under attack. My African American VP for student services, who was responsible for the increased student enrollment, was the one who received the harshest criticisms from faculty. Many white faculty complained that the VP had recruited too many students. For the record, the campus capacity was 10,000 to 12,000 students; we had enrolled only approximately 7,200. When I first became president, many buildings were boarded up due to a lack of students. The college was hugely overstaffed. As a matter of fact, my first month on the job, I was ordered by the chancellor to terminate 26 administrators, despite the fact that we were paying faculty to teach as few as five or six students in many classes. As mentioned above, the high enrollment enabled faculty salary increases. But the student enrollment increase had become a minor detail and faculty raises, an overstated one. A huge increase in student attendance was now burdensome.

�֎ The Moment

In every presidency, there comes what I call a cataclysmic moment. For example, your cataclysmic moment can be when enrollment reaches a tipping point; it booms or bursts, capital campaigns succeed or fail, expected financial gifts become greater or diminish, plans come together or don't. At that moment, because of a sacred spark, something happens. At the beginning of my fourth year, I was feeling confident. I had introduced and received state funding for a $50 million building, cleaned up the campus and received a city beautification award to prove it, increased the budget from $9 million to $30 million, increased salaries (by 100 percent in some cases), and increased enrollment by 74 percent. Even though negativity was swirling in the air, you'd think that in the midst of all the good, what could possibly go wrong? I now realize that is exactly when the moment comes, when you least expect it, when you are full of self-congratulations and not paying attention.

There was a party given at the faculty senate president's home. Approximately 25 to 30 people attended. There were a few administrators and staff, but no African Americans were in attendance. Sometime during the course of the party, the bright idea of a vote came up. I received a vote of no confidence from about 20, six voted against, and two abstained. The results that the majority of faculty had voted no confidence were called in to the local paper. It didn't matter that it wasn't the majority of all faculty, that it was at a party, that it was not a senate meeting, or that all of those present were not faculty representatives. The news hit the papers the next day. The story would not go away. It reached the chancellor's office several hundred miles away. After a few weeks, I received a call from the chancellor's office. I was given a casual choice — that's how it is done in the South, sedately, by innuendo, and not in your face — from the chancellor's assistant to either endure or take a position in the chancellor's office. The chancellor who hired me had died, unexpectedly, a few months earlier. The new chancellor didn't know me nor did I know or trust him. I felt like I had no allies. My moment had arrived and I took the deal.

There is an appropriate time to go, to fall on your sword. I thought it was my time. I was hired in another state as president the following spring. I didn't like going through the madness. Yet those memories are also indelibly imprinted in my brain. While you are going through it and soon after it's over, you replay the refrain repeatedly, thinking maybe I could have done something different; maybe if I had done this instead of that; maybe. . . . maybe. In my head, I knew that race was the issue all along. I don't think that could've been ignored. I suppose, I could have fired the VP early. I could have chosen not to fight about the salary increases. However, had I selected any of these alternatives, I would have been neither happy nor, what I consider responsible. I made the right decisions. I chose my battles correctly. I had my moment.

▓ Lessons

I learned that presidents must have a healthy dose of paranoia. I would advise selecting wise counselors, but guarding your thoughts. Be careful about what you say and to whom you say it. Be cheerful, bold, and courageous. Make small movements, but move judiciously, expeditiously, and always with great caution. It's easier to make small corrections if needed. Hold and exercise high standards, and follow them. Be ethical, moral, and honest. Be above suspicion. Be as discreet as one of Caesar's wives. Above all else, stand for something. Keep students first. Help others when you can. Remember that no one can shield you from your personal stupidity.

Negotiate the salary you want going in, because increases while you are in the job are hard to win. It's most uncomfortable to argue over just desserts because boards can be fickle. There may come a time when exit is your only solution, so be prepared for it. You don't need a reason to exit other than you know that it's time to go. Plan an exit strategy before it becomes necessary. Look for positive reasons to leave. Write three letters entitled as follows: Letter of Resignation (for your boss), Letter of Accomplishments (for newspapers, board, chancellor, and community) and Letters of Application (potential employers). Create a sincere and brief story about the vote for job interviews. Practice your story so that it's canned but doesn't sound like it, understandable, and uncomplicated. The search committees already have Googled you, so be truthful and straightforward. I don't recommend taking media interviews when leaving a job unless you're retiring. That way, there's nothing on the record from you. Have the search committees hear from you firsthand, and do not come across as a victim.

Recognize as early as possible when you're on a path different from that of your college. Either change your path or change to another institution. Be surprised and grateful when you transform people and even more surprised and grateful when you observe the slightest change in institutional culture. I once heard Former Secretary of Education Donna Shalala say, "Changing an institution is like turning a battleship in the middle of the ocean with your bare hands." Shalala isn't saying that creating change in an institution is impossible, just close to impossible. Try to create changes even when it appears to be impossible. Start by looking for reasons to be complimentary at every level all the time.

Finally, take care of your health and your family. When all others fall away, your health and family will be all that are left. Stay close to home. They are on this ride with you, so help them enjoy all the glitz and glamour of the experience. Do not, I repeat, do not bring the workplace home with you. Try to find humor in everything, especially in your disappointments. Make a difference in the lives of everyone with whom you come in contact, especially students, and have fun!

11

WHEN UNCERTAINTY REIGNS

The college had never had a person of color ascend beyond the role of dean of students. The notion of an African American president was not only novel, it was revolutionary. Apart from this development, the system was in transition from several independently accredited colleges with one board to a single accredited system. The new hiring chancellor for the system had come in with many and frequent initiatives, several that challenged the traditional wisdom of community college teaching. He also subscribed passionately to learning college principles. The tradition and unique culture of each college was in conflict with the notion of a multi-campus, single college.

Change was in the air and uncertainty reigned.

"Dr. G." had paid her dues, or so she thought: twenty-plus years of experience, fifteen at the dean level and beyond. Experience in four-year and two-year institutions, and the public sector, along with sufficient fundraising background, satisfied all of the established and conventional requirements. The former president of her campus had practiced what some might consider an imperial presidency, seldom leaving his office. During his ten-year tenure, the college had maintained a flat or slightly decreased enrollment pattern with few innovations. The college management staff was not culturally diverse and was heavily male-dominated. Nonetheless, Dr. G.'s first year as the incoming leader was successful and she was able to make several key cabinet-level appointments. Over a period of eighteen months, she increased diversity significantly to approximately fifty percent at the senior staff level and by ten percent in the faculty ranks.

The changes were profound with impact, beginning a shift in the culture of the college, if not the system. The college seemed to warmly receive the president, if not some of her appointments. Her relationship with faculty was excellent, and the president was known to manage while walking around the campus. She visited classes, had coffee in faculty and staff lounges, and routinely ate in the cafeteria. She attended student events, student and faculty recitals, athletic events and departmental holiday parties. Dr. G. routinely met with representatives of the collective bargaining units, student government, and faculty senate, and held open forums for any and all to voice concerns or make recommendations. It was a textbook, almost fairy-tale, presidency for four or five years, and perhaps one that created a false sense of security about her position.

The undercurrent of unrest with small pockets of disgruntled faculty and staff on all the campuses (but primarily at one of the most conservative locations) had created an almost invisible divisiveness. Governance issues between one of the other presidents and the faculty senate began to spill over to each campus. The chancellor, who had hired both Dr. G. and another minority president, was under siege by the same factions. Inter-campus rivalries and competition only added fuel to the smoldering fire, but Dr. G. believed that her situation was secure because almost none of the issues resided on her campus, or again,so she thought. Little did she know that the very foundation of the system was being quietly undermined. Downsizing had occurred a few months earlier, and several executive-level positions at the campuses had been eliminated. Apparently, this added to the surge of subterranean unrest.

The chancellor's initiatives had brought national recognition to the system. As it turned out, this was more attention than some members of the board were comfortable with because they assumed that increased scrutiny would accompany it. The county government heavily influenced the board, and was anti-college administration. In fact, the county frequently reached the border line of interfering with daily operational matters, and the chancellor often publicly resisted what he considered undue influence. Yet, Dr. G. assumed that her performance was above reproach.

Late in the fifth year of her presidency, a startling announcement was made. The hiring chancellor would be leaving in six months and the remaining executive staff, including presidents, were given the option of renegotiating contracts for one year or potentially being sent home for the eighteen-month remaining duration of their original contracts. The chancellor's cabinet was shocked and dismayed, and Dr. G. was the last to renegotiate her terms. Several weeks later, she had recovered from the disillusionment and was earnestly looking for new professional opportunities. She always hoped that things would return to "normal," but they never did. Starting a new position at 52 was risky, uncertain and filled with incalculable challenges.

As she mulled over her options, the notion that she had done nothing wrong continually plagued her. And then it happened: Dr. G. became fully engrossed in the "It's not my fault" syndrome. Why should she give up her position? She thought long and hard about riding it out. She still could not get past the fact that others on the cabinet, who didn't look like her, seemed to be rather secure in the new contractual environment. Was it discrimination, self-doubt, or a combination of things that had put her in this predicament? Was it divine intervention and fate, or had she really failed to keep an adequate and accurate pulse of the college community? And why did it appear that everybody else took things so calmly? After all, the Anglo males appeared to be in favorable positions, and the Anglo females were seemingly buttressed. The Latino and African Americans had been most visibly impacted, while undercurrents of racism rippled across the system. In the span of six months, a significant percentage of African Americans resigned. The bus was leaving the station. Dr. G. had considered staying at the college for, at least, five more years and perhaps through retirement, however, that was not to be the case.

Over the next couple of months an old adage from one of her senior doctoral professors began to resound in her head: "Manage what you control." This mantra became the operating philosophy for her pursuit of other options.

She decided that she would not let the board, administration, or county government determine her fate and that she would seek and secure a position of her choice, on her own timetable. She established a set of criteria for the type of position, location, and time frame she desired. Dr. G. also used the internet extensively to compare and analyze cost-of-living ratios from across the country, as well as housing and transportation options. She was clearly going to be in charge of her destiny. Within a period of nine months, she had made the finals for four positions and had secured two offers. Neither of the offers was exactly what she was looking for, but each had attractive elements and long-term potential. Dr. G. made the transition to a large, urban district in the system's main administrative office. She anticipated staying there no longer than five years and assumed that she would apply for another presidency.

Controlling one's destiny was important to Dr. G. She believed and practiced principles of self-regulation that included: saving for the proverbial rainy day, working periodically with an executive leadership coach, and staying active with caucuses, and civic and fraternal organizations. She also was an active presenter at state, regional, and national conventions. The high visibility from these presentations and speeches had served her well during her presidency, and there was no reason that they would serve differently in the future.

It's four years later now and Dr. G. has applied for six or seven presidencies in the past two years. She was a finalist two times and a semifinalist twice, but, so far, another presidency has eluded her. She often wonders whether she will ever get another opportunity. Dr. G. knew instinctively when to leave her previous post. She saw the signs and determined that it was in her best interest to move on. Unfortunately, many executives of color fail to read the tea leaves or see the storm coming. What are some of the factors that cloud their discernment? Are there specific skills or techniques that can be used to assess and forecast when it's time to go? How do we recognize and employ them? The "chocolate truth" is that every situation is different, but the signs should be evident if we have our beacons in place.

This discussion can set the framework for a series of training seminars or modules for newly appointed and aspiring presidents and college executives. The very future of persons of color in executive roles may well be determined based on the development of a set of tools for this purpose. The Presidents' Roundtable's Thomas Lakin Institute for Mentored Leadership can be a conduit for the development of this tool kit.

Reflections

When I was a young child, I wanted to be a lawyer. I am not sure if I was influenced by television or if it was because a lawyer in my neighborhood became a judge, founded a law firm, and later sold it for $25 million. Then I met Dr. Bill Banks. This gentleman was erudite and polished, spoke several languages and read a minimum of four newspapers a day, including the Wall Street Journal and New York Times. He was my middle-school history teacher and he wanted to be president of a college. Dr. Banks had degrees from Harvard, Princeton, and Johns Hopkins. And, most of all, he was black. He would admit to me, occasionally, that, with all his academic preparation, it had still been difficult for him to get a tenure track position at a college. It was, after all, the 60's and opportunities were not abundant. Dr. Banks frequently assigned me extra work and made me read boring newspapers from other states and countries, exposing me to different perspectives from around the world. I initially hated the articles – and him – but came to really appreciate and value his mentoring.

Much later, by happenstance, I got a position at a college and the journey began. After five years, I was a dean of students, and fifteen years later, at age 44, a college president. My view of the presidency was an imperialistic one: I was president and everyone needed to understand that. I made the calls and needed counsel from no one, except perhaps, occasionally, the board chair. Then, at the beginning of summer classes, the board chairman walked into my office with his head hung. He looked up at me and said that the board had held a special meeting the previous night (though this was against state law) and voted not to renew my contract. I couldn't breathe for what seemed like five minutes. I asked what the problem was, and he would only say, "The board believes it's in the best interest of the college for you to step down." I could stay at the college as a tenured professor, a benefit I had negotiated as part of my contract; I could accept a buyout, or I could exercise my legal rights. Obviously, I needed to keep working and, the more noise I made, the less likely I was to receive new offers and options. No shortage of advice was available. I consulted with lawyers, colleagues, management texts and resources. I Googled, Tweeted, LinkedIn, and sought other online assistance from leadership coaches.

It was too little too late. I finally realized that my leadership style was incompatible with the college's culture; really any college's culture. But even though someone had to take the fall, I was certain it wasn't going to be me. I suspected a number of disgruntled employees had gotten to their friends on the board to influence it against me. This was a small town and many on the board were neighbors of the college's employees. I had several run-ins with faculty and staff over compensation, teaching load and benefits, not to mention the dismal success rates of our students, particularly students of color. Twice in one semester, shouting matches had erupted between faculty senate leaders and me over reorganization and new faculty appointment issues. One of these meetings concluded in a statement from a faculty leader specifically citing what he perceived as shortcomings being related to my race. The senate quickly censored the faculty member, but I always felt that he simply said what a lot of others were thinking.

I embraced who I was as a minority male and openly celebrated Kwanzaa, Juneteenth, and MLK's birthday. I also recognized and celebrated all the other holidays and/or acknowledged special days or events significant to the college. Frequently, I felt that my sensitivity to others was not adequate to satisfy them, and I rarely was invited to the Lion's Club or Chamber of Commerce events held at private homes. My biracial wife and I often got stares from both African Americans and Anglos when we traveled or appeared together. We had learned to live with this, or at least, to ignore it as best we could, but I always thought it was being held against me at some level.

There are a great number of sources that attribute leadership failure to organizational type and personal-fit disconnects. Organizational culture is invisible and nameless, and assumes no responsibility, yet acts are committed in its name. People hide behind it, but no one is held responsible for its impact or influence on decisions that disenfranchise or diminish others. I made hard decisions, held people accountable, and kept my distance from ascribed and appointed campus influentials. In the final analysis, it was this culture of practices and mores that mightily contributed to my failure. I would not kiss the pope's ring. Faculty had ruled the roost and had influence and unencumbered access to the board; certainly not blameless in this mess. I had been appointed by a six-to-three vote. Several members of the board had never supported me, and one had vowed to get rid of me from day one (she later became acting president for several months). I constantly reminded the board that their fiduciary and stewardship responsibilities began and ended at the policy level and did not include the day-to-day operations of the college. Changes I proposed in my cabinet were always challenged and twice, previously, the board was split five-to-four and six-to-three about major components of my tenure. The third time appeared to be the "charm."

With the exception of a couple of civil rights groups, the community seemed to be ambivalent about my arrival, tenure, and prospective departure. Although I had worked tirelessly to build bridges with the business community, it only resulted in a few invitations to advisory boards and fewer donor resources. It was clearly a conspiracy against me. The board often compared my success with that of the former president who hailed from the area and still operated a family business there. I never had a real chance to succeed. I could have made it if I had been given a fair opportunity, but I could never fit in on the campus or in the community. My family and I often felt like captives on a long leash.

I decided to stay on as a tenured professor and special board advisor. I taught two classes and wrote several position papers for the board. After a couple of years, this grew old, so I was in the hunt again. I recently took a job as president of a medium-sized technical college in the Midwest about forty miles from Chicago. I've learned a lot over the past few years. I have modified my behavior and become more open to advice and recommendations from staff. The difficulty in receiving criticism, lack of sufficient emotional intelligence, and ego are still there, but better managed. Developing awareness is an invaluable pointer in comprehending what's happening to you, not some great while later, but as it happens, in the heat of the action. Awareness is a vital attribute to leadership. It allows you to exercise – in the moment – adult choices about what to do next. You re-gain control and are able to act responsibly.

Contrast this with a less aware response. You forfeit much of your potential and become victim to your own pre-programming. You repeat past patterns of engagement and, as a result, the scene may play out in familiar, but ineffective and possibly quite damaging ways. Leadership insight creates emotional awareness about your identity. It identifies your normal, reflexive emotional patterns, both those that drive you to be good at what you do and those that trigger you, negatively. This awareness helps you understand how and why the patterns were formed and how and why you must assume responsibility for them. The isms will always exist (cronyism, racism, nepotism, etc.). You can't control them, but you can control your responses and develop the ability to deal with them successfully.

12

TO BE OR NOT TO BE AN INSIDE APPLICANT: THAT IS THE QUESTION

The tendency, if you're seeking to move up in a leadership capacity, is to look for an opening within your own institution. While that is a safe option, it is not necessarily the wisest. "Why?" you ask. There are a number of pluses and minuses. Of course, there are many reasons why you would desire to stay put: You know the people, you know the campus, and (assuming that you get the position) you don't even have to physically move anywhere except to another office, maybe in another building. Although it is, perhaps, the most logical and professionally familiar route, moving up within your current institution carries with it many considerations.

First of all, you already have history – good or bad. Part of that history is your past work performance. If you have been doing your job properly, you have had to make some hard-line decisions and there will be some who don't agree with whatever was done (you can't please everyone). Typically, the most disgruntled employees will already have found a way to be planted on the interview committee for your new position so they can make sure that whoever is selected is someone who shares their perspectives. On the other hand, if you haven't made any tough decisions, there are those who will also be upset, since they wanted the dice rolled in their favor during your tenure. The campus dynamics are such that being an inside person is probably both an asset and a hindrance at the same time.

It has been said that timing is everything. When an opening occurs, the time-honored question is, "To be or not to be" an applicant? The answer is complex. Have you been asked to apply by your supervisor or others in authority? If the answer is yes, I hope you have asked why. Is it because you have made some tough decisions in the past? Have you helped your boss look good, or supported him or her during a trying time? Or is it simply that there is no one more logical who should apply? Now, perhaps your co-workers have suggested that you apply. Again: Why? Is it because they want to maintain the status quo for themselves or for their work environment, and they believe that you'll make things easy?

Then, of course, there may be no internal invitations or suggestions that you apply. So what do you do? You could talk with your supervisor regarding what he or she wants to see in the applicant, and what it is that they want the successful candidate to do or change. During this discussion, gauge the supervisor's receptivity to your possible application. At one point in my career I was thinking about a position, but when I met with my supervisor to talk about his move to fill the vacancy, he indicated that he felt another person was ideal for the job. That told me this would probably not be a position that I would get if I applied. If you are serious enough, you may choose to share your career path with your supervisor, but remember that this, too, is risky.

Once you decide to apply, realize that your candidacy will become known. You can choose to tell others (not a good idea) or you can keep it quiet. Regardless, know that people are lining up on both sides: to compete with you for the position, and to sit on the team that makes the decision. At least, one of those who reports to you in your current position will be on the interview committee. In most cases, you will have to deal with the fallout if you don't get the position.

About nine out of ten times, you'll get an interview – there is this unspoken rule that inside candidates are considered and, in some cases, the inside applicant will be advanced to the finals not because he or she is the best, but because the interview committee members can always say they wanted you, but higher-ups did not. It can all be very political. But back to the interview itself: You will have to sell yourself and not assume that anyone in the room really knows who you are. It is important that you be honest and not take credit for things you didn't achieve; and be careful not to present an image of yourself that's inconsistent with your day-to-day demeanor. Remember that those on the committee have worked with you over the years and can easily tell other members the truth.

So, say that you have passed all the hurdles and you get the job. Now comes the real work, because the tendency is for individuals at the organization to expect the same old you. You will have to do something immediately to detach yourself from your previous position. Meet with your current staff to thank them for their support, and then meet with your new staff to set the tone. You should immediately move your operation to another physical space. Within a relatively short period, you need to start to see your organization through new eyes. If you were new to the college you would have about a year to get to know the environment, but as an inside candidate, the "learning curve" excuse does not cut it. Adding to this is that you have to be careful who you ask for assistance.

On the flip side, if you're looking for a new job at a new site there are multiple advantages. Your application is private and it's within your control to disclose until you're granted a final, public interview, or reference-checking occurs. You come to the job with little to no prior baggage (though there will be some unofficial background checking on you). During the interview you can speak more candidly and honestly about who you are and what you have done, even brag about your accomplishments without concern about the opinions of committee members who already know your work record. Then, once you get the job, you're only viewed in your new role, as the people in the new organization won't know you from any past position. And, of course, the other benefit is that you can take your time learning the organization and asking for help, as this is expected. You can also glean interview experience without impacting your current working relationships.

But more importantly, your career trajectory can be faster when you open yourself to outside opportunities. In most cases, you can start to look for a next step upwards after about three years. You can also be a little more daring and even stretch higher than one level above your current job. Typically, turnover is slow within the ranks of organizations, but there are always more options outside of your institution. And the final plus of going outside is the level of experience that you can glean as you move around. If you only know one organization's culture, you have a tendency to see whatever's being done as the only way to do it. Moving to other campuses let's you see different approaches, learn new strategies and build a wider core of friends and colleagues.

On a more personal note, early in my career I almost applied for a promotion where I was working, but someone who understood the down side talked me out of it. Later, I got a job at another college and have since seen the value of being an adventurer. I have worked in California, Texas, Michigan and Florida. My experiences are varied, having worked in states with collective bargaining, shared governance plus systems, districts and single-college institutions. My upward track has been consistent and the time frame at each job has been short (three to four years), by today's standards. Of course, that is my story, and you will have to decide for yourself: To be or not to be an applicant? That is the question.

❈ PART FIVE

THE LIFE OF A LEADER

Culture and the Colonized Mind

Managing the Threesome: You, Your Significant Other, and Your Blackberry

Life Under the Microscope

When is a perk not a perk?

Little Lens or Big Lens

13

CULTURE AND THE COLONIZED MIND

A word of caution to the reader: Do not get this twisted. This is not a scholarly presentation laced with the most current research on leadership. Rather, the intent of this narrative is to draw on my rich blend of education (formal and informal), life, and professional experiences to promote understanding of what it is to serve as a community college president from an African-centered perspective. This body of experiential knowledge will also be framed within an African-centered context. Thus, in reverence to our ancestors and elders who have gone before us, and on whose shoulders we stand, I have sprinkled this narrative with relevant quotations of elder wisdom.

"Get some fat on ya head and nobody can take it from you."

🞧 On Education and Culture

For the purpose of this narrative, education is defined as: the sum total of one's learning experiences throughout the duration of his/her existence, from the womb to the tomb. This definition acknowledges that education is a continuous, life-long process. Furthermore, because the process of education occurs in a social context, this life-long exercise heavily influences worldviews and perceptions of reality. Instructional moments gained through life experience mold frames of reference and analytical processes. I grew up in Texas in the 50's and 60's, so my lenses have been tinted by a series of social realities, such as Jim Crow, the struggles for civil and human rights, and the violence that was associated with racial injustice and oppression. After the deaths of my biological parents, I was raised by extended family members. Murdeer and Cutin Aaron were my first primary life instructors. They were God-fearing, pride-filled elders who preached the importance of education.

This dynamic duo did not compromise on the fundamental principle of learning. They believed, "Do it right the first time so you don't have to lick that calf again." Despite having accumulated a total of just eight years of formal education between them, they were literate, fairly well-read, and had a firm understanding of historical, social, and political issues. They would say, "Colored people ought to know what is going on in their community and around the world. Ain't no excuse for ign'ance." If you asked them a question, they would tell you, "Go look it up and come back and tell me the answer." The Bible, newspapers (national Negro press and local news) and the World Book Encyclopedia were their major sources of information. When our television worked, Murdeer and Cutin Aaron were consistent news and educational journal watchers (i.e. Walter Cronkite's "You Were There" and Edward R. Murrow's "See It Now"). They worked long careers in the service industry as a culinary artist and a sanitary engineer (you know what these fancy titles really mean – I'm just trying to keep your attention!), but these humble people were my teachers, along with a host of other community and church elders. Their teachings would lay the foundation and serve as the framework for my views on culture, leadership, and organizational dynamics. The elders' ability to embrace change, to persevere against any odds, and to value service to others are the attributes that have contributed to my sense of what an educational leader must possess to effectively lead a community college. The formal training I received from higher education validated their wisdom and provided the theoretical basis to enhance my skills set in these disciplines.

"If you don't know where you been, you ain't got no sense of where you can go."

Know Thyself

In this narrative, culture will be defined as a system of beliefs and values that influence the way people and organizations do the things they do. The concept of culture, however, has a myriad of interpretations. This is particularly true when you consider individual cultural background, organizational culture, and the implications of these cultural interpretations on leadership. Culture is the engine that drives the rhythm of an individual; for example, my vivid recollection of Jim Crow is that this social isolation tool created separate realities in which various ethnic groups operated in ethnically homogenous environments. While these separate realities were by no means monolithic, ethnic homogeneity provided a common point of identification.

On the other hand, history is heavily laden with events involving members of these separate realities crusading for cultural and social dominance. The historical and cultural development of the human family is very intriguing and dynamic. This collective narrative serves as a backdrop for understanding how we see the world and how we structure organizations to achieve large-scale work in our society.

"When you gets a bunch of folks together, it's gon' be some mess."

Organizations, such as community colleges, have their own unique cultures, consisting of beliefs and values that influence the way these institutions get things done. College policies and procedures set a standard for expected behavior and the sanctions for any deviations from the norm. The life of the community college is interpreted through the different lenses of educational leaders and administrators. Diversity in the learning environment makes for a rich blend of cultural flavors and experiences. When diversity is acknowledged and appreciated, cultural sharing peaks. When the value of diversity is dismissed, cultural conflict is inevitable. This is true in the community as well. Educational leaders and administrators in the community college setting play a huge role in the development of organizational culture.

"Ain't nobody gonna follow you if you don't know where you goin'."

"It ain't where you been, it's where you goin'."

✠ Leadership and Organizational Culture and Dynamics

One hundred forty-five years ago, President Lincoln signed the Emancipation Proclamation. In this short span of time (compared with how long people of African descent were held captive in America), Africans in the United States have made some great contributions to this country. On the other side of this, the reality is that because of this short history, a significant number of African American community college presidents share a similar status with African American community college students: Like first-generation college scholars, we are first-generation in the field of higher educational leadership. In our recent arrival to the realm of executive leadership, we've encountered challenges similar to the challenges that our students experience. The most pronounced challenge is learning to navigate and negotiate the organizational culture of the college in order to be successful. As presidents, we have much more latitude in this transaction because, to a large degree, we are the stewards of this organizational culture. Nonetheless, just like among students, any action taken in poor judgment, within the context of the organizational culture, could prove to be injurious to our success.

Understanding organizational culture is critical and cannot be underestimated. African Americans are ascending to executive leadership positions at a very interesting time in the evolution of community colleges. Legislative and external agency accountability campaigns continue to escalate. A recessive economy, state funding cuts, and the questionable efficacy of public schooling in developing students' basis skills all create heavy demands on the workforce. This is just a cursory environmental scan of what makes community colleges interesting in this best and worst of times. Given these economic and socio-political realities, the vitality of these open-access institutions is contingent upon creating organizational efficiencies. To achieve organizational efficiencies, contemporary African American community college presidents will have to understand how to guide others through a process of changing the organizational culture. This dynamic process has to be driven by a set of internalized values and beliefs that can withstand the fear of change and passive-aggressive pushback by "haters."

Clinically speaking, some African Americans have mastered the art of functional schizophrenia in order to cope in a society marred by racism and systemic inequities. I confess that I have not been remediated in this skill set. Given their struggles, those who've gone before us paid the cost for this generation to be the boss of its own destiny. Over the years, I have struggled with aligning my leadership values with the Nguzo Saba, Dr. Maulana Karenga's African-centered value system most commonly associated with Kwanzaa. I refer to this process as being a "struggle" because it has taken a lot of trial and error to integrate these basic principles into a traditional leadership frame of reference at predominantly Anglo institutions. The struggle is never-ending and always challenging because of the heterogeneity associated with a diverse workforce. The Nguzo Saba's seven principles serve as the tenets on which I base my team-building strategies, coaching, and change-management tactics. Here is how I apply each principle:

Umoja (meaning "unity") is imperative to achieving the shared vision of the college. Everyone must be a team player.

Kujichagulia (meaning "self-determination") develops clarity of mission as the key to identifying strategies for change within the college.

Ujima (meaning "collective work and responsibility") strives to see everyone committed to collaborating and working toward the common good.

Ujamaa (meaning "cooperative economics") requires that cooperative financial strategies be incorporated to achieve the goals of the college. Wealth accumulated is to be shared. Nobody does without.

Nia (meaning "purpose") translates into achieving outcomes. Keep your eyes on the prize.

Kuumba (meaning "creativity") requires creative approaches to program design and problem-solving. There's more than one way to skin a cat.

Imani (meaning "faith") demonstrates respect for people's ability to contribute to achieving the desired outcome.

Incorporating these African-centered values affords me the opportunity to transcend the confusion that tends to occur when people are "gaming" in a culturally diverse workforce. Promoting these universally applicable social constructs also helps to achieve balance in the professional environment. Given that the life expectancy of African Americans tends to be shorter than that of our Anglo counterparts, staying true to the teachings of Ma'at, the Egyptian principles, is also value added in the workplace.

Another manifestation of fusing an African-centered cultural values orientation into my leadership is the promotion of "democratic cultural pluralism," a concept coined by the late Dr. Asa Hillard. The basic premise of this concept rests on the assumption that distinct, diverse cultures can co-exist if members of each culture recognize the legitimate right of members of the other culture to experience integrity and a sense of justice. This tenet is the core of pluralism. The synthesis of cultural values into my leadership lens promotes a common set of beliefs and values that defines expected organizational behavior. This fusion also sets the parameters for culturally diverse team members to reach a consensus on how they will strive to reach a shared vision. Transforming organizational cultures can only be achieved through changing the value orientation of people. African American community college presidents have inherited an array of organizational challenges, but despite these challenges, our historical and cultural development makes us uniquely qualified to thrive in the dynamic educational environment of community college.

"Don't get caught up in the crab-in-the-bucket game."

"Work hard and don't let nobody pull you down to their level."

✠ Closing Observations for African American community college presidents (or aspiring ones and generations yet unborn)

African Americans are still heavily influenced by ancestral tribalism and the side effects of the long days of our captivity and colonialism. We distrust each other. We hold each other to high, arbitrary standards. When we see a sister or brother in a position of authority, we have unrealistic expectations and perceive him or her as a messiah. This perception carries the expectation that he or she is supposed to follow the black agenda and right all the wrongs of past history. But let this "messiah" disagree with us, or not do what we expect within the designated timeline – a timeline (usually yesterday) that we don't even think about imposing on extended human-family members – and it's "on like Donkey Kong." Get ready for the beat-down!

These descriptors are associated with colonized minds or self-hatred symptoms. As leaders, we must be aware of these socio-psychological dynamics and not be drawn into engaging in a narrow-minded, self-serving "black agenda" game. It is imperative that, as leaders, we never indulge in the acceptance of mediocrity from anyone. Keep your expectations even-steven for everybody and you will avoid the professionally dangerous perception of giving preference based on skin color.

> *"Your word is your bond."*
> *"Do not promise anything you can't deliver."*
> *"Don't mess with Mr. Charlie's prope'ty."*
> *"Don't get caught with your hand in the cookie jar."*

Keep the financial side of the college in order and "in the black." No matter how high we climb in the organizational food chain, we are not exempt from stereotypes about our managerial skills. Don't do anything that will put you in court with the judge ready to take away your dreams, if you know what I mean.

"Hire folk who share your principles and got mo' fat on they head than you."

Always build a team that is loyal, will complement you, and that can fill gaps in your skills set.

"You ain't so slick you can't take another greasin'."

Plan to learn something new each year and stay current on the latest research in your craft.

14

MANAGING THE THREESOME: YOU, YOUR SIGNIFICANT OTHER, AND YOUR BLACKBERRY

The time is 12:45 a.m. on a back-to-work Monday morning. I am gently nudged awake by my lovely wife. As I slowly gain focus and recognize the time, my heart starts to pound because, like me, my wife loves her sleep. For her to be waking me up out of my slumber at this ungodly hour, something has to be terribly wrong. She says in that tone married and formerly married couples know, "Your phone is buzzing." She did not look happy. In fact, she looked positively pissed or in the words of the late, great comedian Robin Harris, she was "pissed off to the highest level of pistivity!"

Like most community college CEOs, I keep my Blackberry on vibrate and every time I get a text message, email, or instant message my phone alerts me with two short buzzes. Because of the 75 to 125 daily emails — not including text and instant messages — the buzzing can be quite irritating. It would be so simple to just turn off my phone when I get home. Yet I'm convinced the first time I do, I'll have that big campus emergency in the middle of the night that for many of us presidents is our worst fear. I definitely do not want to have to explain to my chancellor and board why I could not be reached. So, I have grown to live with the buzzing in the middle of the night. Because you can't assume that every message sent in the middle of night is a message of low priority this muddies the water and sometimes, makes it hard to relax.

Back to 12:45 a.m. when I was awoken with the words, "Your phone is buzzing." While those were the exact words she used, in her tone I clearly heard, "Who in the hell is calling you this time of night?" Lying in bed — dead tired — I check my voicemail, using the speakerphone feature to hear the voice of a woman I met two years prior. She was calling to express her interest in a newly posted position at my campus. But before my wife could utter a word, I immediately called back and said, "I appreciate your interest in the college, but this is my mobile phone and please refrain from using it again." Embarrassed and apologetic, she explained my office number was not working. This was true. Nine months prior, my institution changed service providers, which meant my previous number was no longer operational.

She went on to explain that, in her haste, she didn't realize the alternative number on my business card was my mobile. I interrupted her and in my most calm and stern voice, replied, "No problem. Again, this is my mobile phone. Good night." I placed my phone back on the night stand and rolled over to make amends, "Good night, Baby." She replied, "Good night," but this time in her tone I heard, "That's right, Baby, put her in check. I love you."

⊠ 24/7 Reality

Twenty-four hours a day, seven days a week: serving as the chief executive officer at a community college can become your life with not much room for anything else. Let me be clear that the job isn't necessarily 24/7 because there are urgent and critical matters that require you to work around the clock. In my opinion, the 24/7 reality exists primarily because of the advances in technology that allow us to access email, text messages, and voice mail at the touch of a button. Because of Personal Digital Assistant communication devices such as iPhones and Blackberries, it's become so easy, and tempting, to stay plugged into the needs and interests of your respective institutions around the clock.

In addition, there are a range of professional activities that require us to stay engaged around the clock. If a student has a negative run-in within the community, or a faculty or staff member faces a crisis, an injury occurs. If you serve in a state with inclement weather, the expectation from students and employees alike is that the campus CEO provides ample notice whether the campus will remain open for business with the threat of snow and ice. You may apply for a grant and find yourself working down to the wire. Fortunately for me, the above situations are not daily occurrences. Nevertheless, the temptation to stay plugged into my Blackberry is an around-the-clock battle.

There may also be legitimate and important volunteer opportunities in your life that require you to work beyond the traditional workday. Personally, I serve on the boards of three national associations: the American Association of Blacks in Higher Education, Presidents' Round Table, and the American Association of Community Colleges. These three national volunteer opportunities do require me to stay plugged in, as we will often find ourselves — due to impossible schedules and time zone — in conference calls at non-traditional times. My role on these boards also sends me out of town frequently, for national meetings and conventions. As you can see, being a part of national boards is a significant factor in the 24/7 equation.

A host of local and regional volunteer opportunities may also require you, as a college CEO, to be engaged beyond the traditional workday. I serve on at least five local boards, community committees, and associations that keep me engaged from early in the morning to late at night. Like most CEOs, I serve on the board of my local Chamber of Commerce, the regional Community Foundation Board, the Economic Development Board, and several other committees that support our area school districts. My involvement in a handful of local and regional community engagement opportunities contributes to the 24/7 reality.

I made a conscious decision to have only one mobile device that is the property of my institution. Many of my more seasoned colleagues, under no circumstances, will agree to have just one mobile. They have one device for personal use and one for the institution. I understand clearly their need to have a separate device for personal use due to the Sunshine Law, which applies to my state, enabling any private citizen to gain access to email, text, and voice messages of a professional device. However, each institution has its own personal use policy. Based on your institution's policy, you can decide if it's critical for you to have multiple mobile communication devices. I personally cannot manage two sets of emails, text or phone messages, and security codes. It's in my best interest to have only one cell phone. When you choose to use an institutional mobile device, you must understand that at any given point in time your phone can be confiscated and your phone records can be scrutinized for inappropriate material sent or received by the institution's device.

Understanding the parameters, I'm careful with my phone and correspondence. I'll never intentionally write an email, text message or leave a voicemail from the institution's mobile device that contains disparaging remarks about anyone or anything. I do not complain over the phone, but rather I use the device to clearly communicate facts. Even during personal use of my phone, I make sure to eliminate typos and avoid using shorthand. I assume that my messages will be reviewed and therefore take extra care, because I'd like to present myself favorably. I strive to maintain a level of professionalism even when corresponding with my wife, friends, and family.

MANAGING THE THREESOME: YOU, YOUR
SIGNIFICANT OTHER, AND YOUR BLACKBERRY

✠ The Doghouse: Getting and Staying Out

Higher education, particularly at the executive level, has historically been a male-dominated industry. Even the faculty ranks are disproportionately staffed with males. However, as our communities become more and more diverse and institutions begin to understand the value of diversity, gender and otherwise, the composition of higher education is shifting rapidly. Nonetheless, women dominate the administrative support staff, such as administrative assistants and clerks. I haven't noticed any changes in this trend and in every institution I've served, I've been surrounded mostly by women. In an environment where you work closely with individuals for a common good or goal, it's natural to gravitate to some individuals more than others. On occasion, you may even find someone attractive. To acknowledge attraction, however, is unacceptable, particularly if you're the campus CEO.

Something valuable that I strongly believe, but had to learn the hard way, is not to ignore any remarks or comments made by my significant other. Spiderman has the "spider sense," but my wife has a sixth super sense. Nine times out of ten, well honestly 9.9 times out of ten, whenever she has a feeling, a notion, or an instinct, she's right. For example, when we've been out with folks I work with or in the community and she tells me things like "I don't like her," or makes observations such as "She was standing a little too close to you," I should always paid attention. In my early days I would brush these things off by saying something like, "We all work together; we're professionals, and you have no reason to be worried."

Today, whenever my wife makes these types of comments, I pay close attention. I suggest you do so as well. More times than not, they are in a position to sense things you cannot. It's much easier to get in the dog house, but very difficult to make your way out. In most scenarios, there's nothing to do in the moment so the best thing is to keep mental notes. Wait to see if your significant other's perceptions match with your experiences. If so, then you may have to clarify the professional boundaries you expect. For instance, I pay close attention to voicemails, email, and text messages and their frequency to determine if these contacts are legitimate correspondences or subtle hints. Once I determine the situation needs to be addressed, I share my concerns with the individual directly. On the surface these types of conversations appear to be difficult, but if you focus on the actions versus the person, it's actually pretty simple and straightforward. When I receive numerous emails or voice messages that seem questionable, I address it directly with the individual by saying something like, "As the leader of this institution, it's important to our success that I retain creditability at all times. Therefore, it's critical that I am not opened up to any unnecessary criticism. I truly believe your intentions are innocent, but from the way this correspondence is written or the number of times you have contacted me concerning subjects that do not seem work-related, a reasonable person could draw the wrong conclusions. It would be greatly appreciated if you would not allow me to be in a situation where my judgment, my values, and my commitment to my wife could be questioned. A response like this, although kind, is very clear, leaving no room for misinterpretation. It also focuses on the actions and not the person, which is very important. In this example, the actions are the problem and not the person so allow the individual to save face and provide clear expectations in going forward.

As an African American man, regardless of what title or position I hold, I have implemented a personal policy that bans flirting. This becomes a critical necessity as a campus CEO. It does not matter if you're married or single, man or woman. As the campus CEO, you cannot afford to leave any room for your actions to be misinterpreted. Although it's obvious to me how important a no flirting policy is for a campus CEO, it was a tough adjustment. I am a Southerner, and we pride ourselves on making the ladies in our presence feel safe, secure, and quite frankly, good. However, I no longer say anything as simple as "Oh, I love that dress!" or "Did you get your hair done? It looks wonderful!" Some might argue that comments like these do not constitute flirting. You must always remember at the end of the day your intent will not matter. What matters, ultimately, is how the people around you interpret your words and actions. Because I do not want to leave any room for misinterpretation, I've instituted a no flirting rule that includes not giving compliments, no matter how innocent.

Even before I was married, I had issues with faculty, staff, and students attempting to interact with me on a personal level. Because I have always had a healthy fear of being falsely accused or labeled, I've always effectively dealt with inappropriate and unprofessional behavior. The best strategy on how to handle this kind of situation was given to me by one of one of my phenomenal mentors. He believed that "the best defense is a great offense." More specifically, he suggested that if one wants to eliminate questionable behavior, one needs to have plenty of pictures of one's significant other whether it is a boyfriend, girlfriend, husband, or wife. If you have children, have pictures of those beautiful kids around your office. Now that I'm married, I can't tell you have powerful it is to have pictures of my children and my spouse in my office. I even carry them in my cell phone. I have a wonderful wife and beautiful children and talking about them definitely deters those who think I may have an interest in them that is beyond professional. We're all human, and it's natural to work with associates we find attractive but under no circumstances can you show any weakness. If you drop your guard, I promise you someone will be skillful enough to exploit your weaknesses.

▓ On the Ground

The role of being a community college CEO is seductive. It's easy to get a false sense of importance. Presidents are led to believe that we are of greater importance than those we serve. Things like presidential parking spaces, country club memberships, and automobile allowances are just a few of the benefits you might receive as a college CEO. When you talk to folks, they will tell you they want their president cared for and treated well. In many cases, presidents are encouraged to live a life synonymous with first class and first class only. For me, however, it's very important to stay faithful to the traditions of my upbringing and values. I believe I'm an important part of my institution's success, but I am just one of many. I have learned to resist the whole notion of people believing and thinking I am more important than I am. If you are not careful and grounded, you will start to believe you are more important than others and should have privileges that others do not. If you allow this to happen to you, I guarantee that this will be the beginning of the end for you. You'll open yourself up to criticism, and you'll be susceptible to falling short of the values and the mission of your institution and your own personal values.

Buying into the notion that you're somehow more important than those you serve could also put your relationships at home at risk. Your arrogance could make it easier for you to dismiss your significant other's concerns if you think that you or the work that you do is of higher importance. In this context, be careful and be intentional, with the objective to gain confidence and trust with your significant other. It's important that you get a sense from him or her about the important and urgent issues impacting your relationship and your family. Let's put it this way: Everything I do is important, but only a few of these important things are urgent. The urgent items are what need my attention first. This little rule enables me to have a little bit of balance in my life.

When I'm at home, I'm plugged-in to my family. I pay attention to my wife and my children and I enjoy the riches life can bring. At the end of the day, the institution I serve has an established history that began long before I got there and will continue long after I'm gone. The sobering truth is that as a campus CEO there will be a device sitting next to your bed beeping, buzzing, or chirping constantly. Just make sure you're not so plugged-in to your institution that you miss sight of the people who want to be with you.

15

LIFE UNDER THE MICROSCOPE

Once appointed to the chief executive officer/chancellor/president position, you become a mirror of your institution of higher learning. When the public sees you, they see the institution you represent; when they see your institution, they also see you.

I have served seven years as president of a campus within a multi-campus, urban, community college system. Although we offer all the traditional transfer degree programs, we have a particular focus on health-related occupational programs. As campus president, there is a litany of internal and external committees, programs, events, and initiatives in which I am expected to participate. Internally, these include but are not limited to: campus/college academic senate meetings, campus/college facility planning committees, executive leadership meetings, president's staff and individual direct reports meetings, Phi Theta Kappa induction ceremonies, student organization activities, and athletic events. Externally, these include, but are not limited to: chambers of commerce events; local, regional, state, and national governmental events; ground-breaking/ribbon-cutting ceremonies; service organization events; K-12 school district events; college/university partnership initiatives; nonprofit organization events including serving on selected governing boards; keynote addresses at various community events; and participating on a host of community panel discussions on multiple topics.

Several years ago, during a visit to a large university my daughter was considering for her undergraduate studies, I attended a dinner hosted by administrators and faculty. As the university president was speaking to the audience, I asked a professor seated next to me how often she had the opportunity to be in the presence of the president. She responded, "This is a bonus tonight as I normally only see him twice per year: at the faculty annual fall kickoff meeting and at commencement." She indicated that the president was so adept at fundraising for the university that his contract extensions were never an issue for the governing board. The professor went on to say that if the faculty unit never saw him, his position would be safe as long as he continued to raise significant external funds. That professor's comments demonstrate how important fundraising is for CEOs of higher education institutions, especially in the current economic climate.

Balancing campus and community expectations can be extremely difficult. As a community college president, there are many demands on your time. I have found a few practices to be very effective in meeting (or more appropriately, attempting to meet) internal expectations. I have my administrative assistant schedule a "Walk the Campus" weekly just as she schedules other meetings for me. During these campus tours, I visit two buildings on campus to ensure sufficient time for discussions with students, faculty, and staff members. I always have a note pad for any follow-up required or commitments made during my walk. Then, within 24 hours, I make every effort to communicate with those who would anticipate my response. This lets faculty, staff, and students know that their input matters to the president. Extending oneself in this manner pays great dividends for a leader.

Another practice that has been very effective for me with the internal community is availing myself to attend most large gatherings of faculty, staff, and students on campus. I do everything possible not to be on vacation, at a conference, attending a meeting at district office, or speaking at a community event when these well-attended campus events are scheduled. It's important to take care of home first.

When dealing with the print media, I've found a very logical and effective process to communicate clearly. Once the interview concludes, I always ask the reporter to read back what they recorded pertaining to the more significant issues discussed. More often than you might imagine, there is one word or a short phrase that was inadvertently mis-recorded or mis-communicated that changes the context or intention of the response. This practice affords the interviewer and the interviewee a great opportunity to correct it.

These strategies, and others, have helped me along the way to embrace my role as the college's Chief Executive Officer. As president, you can never forget your role. Wherever you go, and whomever you speak with, remember that you are always representing the students and faculty of your community institution.

16

WHEN IS A PERK NOT A PERK?

Finally I have arrived. I have an assigned parking space. No more circling the lots looking for a spot. I can just drive right in and park. One year later, I realize that this is not a perk. "What happened," you ask? Well, let me explain...

I have seen administrators in the midst of a major crisis over what could initially be seen as rewards for receiving administrative positions. As you know, in most positions you work long hours, including weekends and evenings, enduring attacks on your character, both on and off campus, so it stands to reason that there'd be some other wonderful goodies to compensate for all that you do. As a gesture, institutions will provide a variety of perks, but beware of the "gift."

Parking is one of those things you might see as harmless and low level. It didn't dawn on me until about the fourth or fifth call from one of my board members when I was off campus. The caller would always say, "I was just calling to check in," but it was always when I was away. Shortly afterward, the board member started accusing me of not being on campus enough (notwithstanding that the assignment the board had given me was to get out into the community). I didn't immediately connect the dots, but I later realized that individuals on the campus were alerting the board member whenever my car wasn't in its reserved spot. Lesson learned! I stopped parking in my space — after all, I was the president so I could park anywhere I wanted. The fallout was amazing. All of a sudden, when people showed up for appointments, they would ask my staff when I would be on campus, or they'd try and reschedule, since I "wasn't there." It was always a surprise when I came out of my office to greet them. Board members would call and my staff would put them through to me. I came to realize that people watched my parking spot to try and measure how hard I was working. I recommend that you not park in your assigned space, especially if it is visible and right in front of the lot.

Another "perk" to avoid is having the use of a vehicle written into your contract. If possible, get a car allowance and drive your own car instead. One of my president colleagues had it written in her contract that she would have access to a car owned by the college. What she did not realize is that the previous president drove a seven-year-old sedan. But she went to the car dealer and bought a high-end, upgraded SUV. This simple transaction didn't start her off well with the faculty. Remember, your detractors are collecting notes as to why you should be let go.

Oh, and then there's the coveted house. What a thrill to live in a home owned and paid for by the college. While this sounds grand, it comes with its own set of hidden problems. Typically, the house is old and needs repairs, or it doesn't reflect your personal taste. Any remodeling will be obvious and discussed afterwards. The grapevine will report that the old bathroom was good enough for the past president, but now the new president is updating it. Picture the press and the headlines about misuse of public dollars. Another down side of having a college-owned house is that everyone knows where you live, when you're home, who is visiting, etc. I've learned that it is better to live several miles from the college so your private time isn't kept under a microscope.

Got a college-issued credit card? Then make sure that you do not use the card for anything personal. I succeeded a president who used his college credit card for personal items. Even though he paid the college back, the purchases were traceable, and this still continues to haunt him. In some cases you can use the card for personal needs, such as meals, but be cautious about ordering elaborate dishes. Eat very modestly and if you have a rare, unusual meal (at an odd time or location), document when and why for your personal records, in case you are ever asked about it.

"Travel expenses" – from airplane and cab rides to hotel stays – are subject to personal interpretation. Bottom line: Be very frugal when using the credit card. Travel economy style and even be cautious about accepting a first-class upgrade offer if there are others from your college or district on the plane. Take the most reasonable transportation to and from the hotel – this is not a time to ride in a limousine. Always stay in the conference or standard hotel rooms and, again, watch your use of room service.

Alcohol consumption, while not a presidential perk, is an area that you should also handle with care. It is best to get a separate tab for drinks and pay for them on your own personal credit card or with your own cash. I would suggest when you are at an event with other college employees that you limit yourself to one drink and, if you have a propensity for getting inebriated and losing control, stay away from any alcohol. Of course, you should never drive when you have had too much to drink. If you're ever arrested while under the influence, the newspaper headlines will focus on your position at the college. In some cases your employer can use this as grounds to dismiss you.

Finally, employing family members or friends in any capacity should be avoided. The "perk" of ability to hire can backfire: One of the college presidents in my home state lost her job over an $800 consulting contract because she gave it to a family member. Always be aware of how your "perks" will be seen by the public and decide for yourself if each perk is really a perk at all.

PART SIX

LEGACY

Mentoring, an Essential Leadership Skill

The Architect of Your Own Destiny

Reflections: the Business of Leading a College

17

MENTORING:
AN ESSENTIAL LEADERSHIP SKILL

My personal and professional journey into the academy was a long and tedious one. I graduated from high school in the early 1970s and was one of the approximate 20,000 children over the age of 18 aging out of foster care. I found myself having to make an abrupt transition to adulthood and independence with little or no assistance from a caregiver, biological family member, or the child welfare system. I had no safety net if I failed to succeed at navigating the adult world.

Though I had role models and graduated from high school with honors, I had no immediate family who had attended college and had no idea that college was even possible. Consequently, I spent many years stumbling through life, working menial jobs, fighting to survive, and raising my son. Finally, tired of struggling, I found my way to the open doors of a community college. I was 27, scared, and broken.

My first encounter as a student at that urban community college was a young African American woman just a few years older than I. After finding me in a back hall crying and trembling, she introduced herself as Mrs. Wyatt, Dean of Allied Health. Though I had no idea of her role, I was nevertheless comforted when she listened as I blurted out my desire to find a job and take care of my son. She spent two hours with me that day, explaining the financial aid and admissions processes. She offered to help me develop a plan of work based on my career aspirations and admissions testing. I can never be sure that if Ms. Wyatt hadn't shown up when she did that I would've enrolled. I was blessed to have met her that day as she ignited within me a new-found thirst for learning and made me believe that, yes, it was possible.

Over the years, Ms. Wyatt and I developed an informal mentoring relationship. She helped me build self-confidence, and strengthened my motivation to continue my education. When I completed community college, I pursued a bachelor's degree in a non-traditional format: evenings and weekends. I did not anticipate going further. However, a mid-level leadership opportunity arose at work whereby I could increase my earning potential and work fewer hours, or so I thought. First, I needed a graduate degree.

My immediate supervisor saw my potential and spoke with senior management. They agreed to promote me while I worked towards a graduate degree in administration and supervision. In record speed, I completed my first master's, and with degree in hand delved head first into leadership. I banged my head hard, not understanding the culture of that particular suburban health care institution. In that environment, I had to learn to be a hard-nosed leader.

The organizational culture dictated an autocratic leadership style in which there was limited or no input from subordinates. The administrator was king or, in my case, queen. I fought to retain as much power and decision-making authority as possible. As a young, unseasoned administrator, I did not invite input nor consult with the more experienced employees in my division. My subordinates were expected to obey orders without receiving any explanations. The reward was not to be pencil whipped into shape. Ruling with iron fists, I got the job done, but it took its toll. I stressed myself and everyone else to the breaking point.

I thought, "If only I had a role model that looked like me," then I might get better results. Instead, I honed my leadership skills by reading every best seller on the market written primarily by white men. I modeled myself after the much older, non-minority males who made up the senior executive team at that institution. I was not prepared for what happened next. The institution went through a restructure and I was the first to go on the lay-off list. On the way out the door they told me that I lacked tact and diplomacy.

Being the tenacious individual that I am, I soon landed another leadership position with a different health care institution. This time my two bosses were both black females. I thought, great, now I'll be supported and become a great leader! I armed myself with information on mentors and scheduled my meetings. Dressed for success in my crisp black suit and pumps with portfolio in hand, I walked into the meeting, gave my introduction, and spouted the benefits of mentoring for both the mentor and mentee. The first sistah reared back in her chair, arms folded and said, "So you want me to help you take my job." I blinked in disbelief, and then I checked to see if she were serious. Her face remained set in place, almost angry. "No," I stuttered, "I just thought that with all of your years of experience you would be willing to help me." "Well," she responded, "I just don't have the time. You are a bright young lady. You'll figure things out."

She must have made a call as soon as I left her office. When I arrived at my next appointment, boss lady number two did not even bother to offer me a seat. In fact she didn't look up from the paper she was writing on. She said tersely, "I don't mentor. Your paycheck is your mentor, your incentive to do your job." I left her office deflated, hurt, and disappointed. Feeling a little sorry for myself after these two meetings, I almost decided to give up. However, my stubborn nature prevailed, and I decided shortly after those two encounters to change professions.

Like a tumbleweed blowing in the wind, I found myself in a second master's program for Adult and Higher Education. My first graduate degree focused on the non-human aspects of administration: budgets, facilities, and the like. This second degree program provided a solid foundation in behavioral and social science. I challenged the traditional model of leadership and power, moving from an individualistic and hierarchical stance to one that was more collaborative. In other words, I no longer had to wield power over others. I learned to acquire power by building relationships and working with others to achieve results. I gained the skills to handle unique and diverse leadership challenges, while obtaining a better understanding of organizational structure. My degree in Higher Education was a catalyst for self-improvement and launched my career in community college leadership.

Life had brought me full circle. Once I graduated, I found employment at a multi-campus urban/suburban community college as a program director for Allied Health. I believed intuitively that my first and only mentor, Ms. Wyatt, who by then had made her transition, had touched me from a spiritual place. I entered the doors of my employer much like when I was a student, scared but ready to absorb all I could, like a sponge.

I developed a career advancement plan that included volunteering for committees and curriculum projects. I continued my education, eventually earning a terminal degree. Still, I wanted to find a mentor to help me chart my career path. The environment was competitive, and many of the African American women who were in positions of leadership had been with the college for a number of years. As an ambitious newcomer, I felt less than welcomed. I tested the waters by bringing up mentoring opportunities over lunch or snuck the topic in during meetings. No one seemed interested. Reasons ranged from competing obligations, to "No one mentored me," to echoes of "You'll figure it out."

The books I had read highlighted several keys to black women's attainment of and perseverance in top-level administrative positions. These included: developing mentor relationships with other black women who aspired to gain senior, executive level positions; leadership skills; engaging in teaching, research, and service; and carving out a distinct career path. "To whom much is given, much is required" had become my affirmation in life. I strongly believed that the availability of appropriate role models was particularly important to African American women because of the discriminatory intersection of gender and race.

Remembering what the African American senior level administrator had told me years before, I did "figure it out." I learned to climb the ivory tower even with bruised knees. I can never discount how important my informal mentoring relationships had been, but I think it may have been easier if I could've walked in the footsteps of an African American woman who had gone before me.

Support from mentors and other experienced administrators are important to the successful socialization of novice administrators. Black female aspiring and current administrators should attend professional development workshops and conferences in order to connect with other black female administrators and develop mentoring relationships. These connections and networks serve as a means to hear about other opportunities in the field, to share ideas, collaborate on projects, teach about appropriate professional behavior and protocol, and offer greater professional visibility.

There is a dire need for black female administrators to accept, support, and promote other women. A network of sympathetic and supportive mentors could share techniques on how to handle tough situations. None of us can work in isolation. Many an aspiring academic administrator has tried and, without an understanding of the unwritten policies of advancement, failed miserably.

The literature supports my experiences, noting that women, especially black women, are not always prepared for leadership due to the lack of role models or mentors in the field. Studies conducted by Patton (2009) and Crawford & Smith (2005) revealed that women administrators experience low levels of organizational commitment due to job ambiguity or lack of clarity about their roles and responsibilities. Both studies mentioned that role ambiguity was a result of the lack of mentoring provided for women aspiring to higher positions in administration.

Female administrators who serve as mentors can often be vague about their jobs and responsibilities. As a result, female mentees are not effectively prepared for the next promotion. These mentees are not given the knowledge and skills to navigate the position. Current statistics reflect the disproportionate number and lack of presence of black women in high-level administrative positions in the academy.

According to the American College President Report (2007), the percentage of female presidents more than doubled, from 10 percent in 1986 to 23 percent in 2006. However, women's progress has slowed in recent years. The proportion of presidents who are racial or ethnic minorities showed a much smaller increase, from 8 percent in 1986 to 14 percent in 2006. When institutions that specialize in serving minority populations are excluded, only 10 percent of presidents are from racial/ethnic minority groups.

It can be argued that I made it into this elite group in spite of not having a mentor to beat the odds, and that is somewhat true. I also think that as a black woman, I was able to persist because of the leadership skills I learned during the most challenging, interesting, and sometimes difficult experiences of life. The home and family served as my first leadership experience. The skills I learned from my foremothers — teamwork, conflict management, balancing multiple priorities, working with scare resources—are important tools for a leader.

Contrary to theoretical debates, I don't think I was born a leader. I agree with Kouzes and Posner (2007) who state in their book The Leadership Challenge, "Leadership is not a gene or a secret code. Leadership is acquired through hard work." True leadership is a set of observable skills and abilities that are shaped through education, practice, role modeling, and mentoring.

I have found that despite opposition related to racism, sexism, unsupportive and unwelcoming work environments, black women must possess certain leadership traits to be successful in their work environments. Regardless of gender, successful leaders must set realistic goals, but also they must push themselves beyond their comfort zones. There has to be a level of self-awareness and soul-searching to know one's own convictions and values. This enables us to clarify principles, be creative, span boundaries, and be risk takers.

As an administrator, I have constantly sought ways to progress as an individual and to improve my work environment. It can be mentally draining and physically exhausting, yet I stay committed, energized, visionary, and productive. Most importantly, I remember my challenges, and I reach back to help others find the leader who, with proper polishing, will emerge in each of us.

I also tell my mentees that they can be textbook perfect leaders and still end up with their heads on the chopping block. When perceived failures happen, we must not be paralyzed by them. Rather we need to harness all of our energy, grab opportunities, and reinvent ourselves. Being a leader is about empowering others to achieve the organization's goals and making a contribution to our communities and society.

Today's world of work is transforming rapidly. The signs of these changes are all around us: emerging technologies, shift in demographics, failing economies, and globalization. As leaders, we must be prepared for change and adversity. If I had to select one trait of a leader in the face of adversity, the true leader has humility and perseverance. We must remain passionate in the face of setbacks and obstacles. We must constantly move from tired to inspired and, most importantly, to be a leader is to serve. What better way to serve than to assist women, people of color, and others who are less favorably positioned within the academy to move into administrative positions. In parting, I would share with any young aspiring administrator words that I once read in *Acts of Faith* by Iyanla Vanzant:

You are growing and learning every moment of every day. Regardless of what you have been told, you can and do change with every new experience. Each experience enhances your capabilities by giving you something new to draw upon. Every new capability you discover and develop leads to a new opportunity. As long as you have the capability and an opportunity, there is a new possibility for you to grow and learn something new. Dare not to limit yourself to only knowing or doing one thing.

Take a chance by putting all you know to use. Accept all invitations to do a new thing and when you do it, celebrate. Move toward your wildest dream, take the labels off your mind, and step boldly into your greatness.

References

Crawford, K. and Smith, D. (2005). —The we and the us: mentoring African American women *Journal of Black Studies*, 36(1), 52-67.

Kouzes, J. and Posner, B. *The Leadership Challenge*. San Francisco: Jossey-Bass. 1995

Kouzes, J. and Posner, B. *The Leadership Challenge Planner*. San Francisco: Jossey-Bass. 2000. Lori Patton. —My sister's keeper: A qualitative examination of mentoring experiences among African American women in graduate and professional schools *The Journal of Higher Education* 80.5 (2009): 510-537.

Available at: **http://works.bepress.com/loripattondavis/12**

18

THE ARCHITECT OF YOUR OWN DESTINY

If someone had told me fifty years ago that I would be book-ending a forty-year career working in community colleges as a founding educator, I probably would have said: "Absolutely no way on Earth." Admittedly, doing something that met all the requirements of a family parable passed from one generation to the next, since the mid-1800's, was inevitable: "You are the architect of your own destiny," my elders would say. Now that is a heavy parable! It was preached so much that I ended up writing it on my bedroom walls while growing up. My Dad always told me, "If you dream it, you can live it. You simply have to plan for it."

I stepped into a community college career, literally, by accident. School was always easy for me. If I was not challenged, I would get bored very quickly. Such was the case as I was finishing a masters program in counseling and awaiting acceptance into medical school. I decided to do a six-week internship at a community college in Oakland, in the San Francisco Bay Area. That was nearly forty years ago and such a natural fit. I have never regretted the switch from med school plans to community college. I was hooked on wanting to transform lives. I saw that, with planning and encouragement, I could help others to help themselves. I took a full-time position as a founding faculty member (counselor and bio-psychology instructor) at a brand new school. For a twenty-two-year-old straight out of college with only six weeks experience as an intern, I had a huge learning curve. While many people would see my lack of knowledge and exposure to the system as an obstacle, I saw it as a challenging opportunity.

Starting a professional career at a brand new institution was like falling into a utopia. I had the rare chance to help create an environment, a culture that would be long-lasting for generations to come. My new colleagues and I melded ideas, dreams, experiences, behaviors, and attitudes into a formula for what we considered a productive college environment. Unfortunately, as new people were brought into this utopia, its characteristics started changing. Growth and development stifled. Clashes became a daily occurrence. Over time, I saw the environment transforming, and I was transforming as well. I needed to expand my horizons, broaden my experiences, challenge my intellect, and satisfy my aspirations as a young professional. Boredom became a constant element. After fourteen years, I knew it was time to move on. Moving on meant taking risks, facing new challenges, and setting new goals. But moving on was not a difficult decision for me because I always embraced change and looked to the next step in my life as another challenging opportunity. Risk-taking is very important. You cannot remain in an environment and expect it to change to fit your needs.

So the next logical step was to move into full-time administration, since I had been tapped to do a variety of administrative chores that full-time administrators decided to delegate to aspiring leaders like myself. However, moving up that career ladder also meant moving out of familiar circumstances. I often asked myself, "Will I ever find another utopia that will satisfy me like my first experience?" Probably a much better question was, "What do I need from my new environment, in order to consider it utopia?"

Off I went into a vast world of community colleges, in search of opportunity and satisfaction. I vowed not to stay long if I detected disruption, corruption, negativity, evil, and intolerance. I sought environments where integrity, acceptance, and tolerance were core values; where people willingly gave so that others could develop, where selfish acts were limited to stealing a mental health day now and then to rejuvenate the adrenalin. After three different and progressively higher-level administrative positions in three college districts, and having uprooted my family physically by relocating for each position, I found a work environment that met my expectations. People were underpaid, but that did not matter to them. The work and environment were, in the eyes of many outsiders, probably the most unimaginable of any place in higher education. Yet, I found my niche, my utopia, again.

At least, I thought so at the time. Becoming a vice chancellor of the largest system of higher education in the world was like being David and taking on Goliath: hard work and beginning many tasks starting at ground zero. Having had experiences in creating and reconstructing environments became great, sellable attributes in my career. Besides, I always accepted positions with a positive attitude and an understanding with my inner spirit that I could either stay on my own terms, or leave on my own terms. I was still the architect of my destiny and I refused to allow others to take that control away from me.

I understood what I needed in a work environment that would support my quest to succeed as a good person, as a quality professional, and I understood what would provide elements that made me feel satisfied and productive. I had to be in an environment that thrived and valued positive work habits and attitudes. My utopia needed to utilize its employees' talents, knowledge, skills, and abilities. A sense of pride and ownership were essential. Quality, efficiencies, and effectiveness were daily goals. In addition, good, clean humor was very important.

I thrived as vice chancellor. I touched the lives of many people within our state system of community colleges. I helped reconstruct the image, integrity, and credibility of student support services and programs. New policies were created, laws changed, and financial resources were pumped into our system at unprecedented levels. Staff that I supervised were tapped for their talents, and respected for their knowledge and experience. Many eventually moved on to become leaders, taking on administrative and CEO positions across the state.

Times were good and I was extremely proud and passionate about the accomplishments of our system. I also understood that, at some point, I would reach a plateau that would ring my boredom bell again. I always knew that I should be prepared before that bell rang. Many people had encouraged me to consider the next level: CEO of a college. It was that next logical step in higher education. I quickly learned, however, that searching for that just-right CEO fit was going to become a nearly full-time job in and of itself. During my search for a presidency, many obstacles appeared, testing my strength and resolve as an African American female. I was hard-pressed to adapt, as I always had, by turning such obstacles into challenging opportunities. I researched college after college, conducting what I called the "good-fit review." I only applied and interviewed at those institutions that met my criteria, taking serious note to avoid programs that appeared to be in need of "diverse" candidates – being

African American and a woman are priceless for recruiters, and I vowed never to become that guinea pig to fulfill a hiring quota. Nope! Not me! I applied and interviewed in three processes, walking away with the thought that any of those institutions could work for me.

A work environment that doesn't fit you will cause problems, tension, and constant sorrow, all elements that can negatively influence and change the entire course of one's professional career. Finding the right fit does not have to be an ordeal if you know your basic requirements. I have always had to make sure the position, the responsibilities, and the environment worked for me, not for others. Ultimately, I was blessed with what I honestly believe to be the best fit and the best job in the entire United States community college system: I became the founding president of a college that did not exist – I was hired to create a college. My utopia! I was given the incredible responsibility to design and develop a program for the twenty-first century, literally from ground zero. My task was to create a culture and environment that included: development of a facilities master plan; a college governance structure and fiscal stability; implementing operations and future endeavors; development and implementation of programs, services, curriculum, and processes; hiring of all faculty, staff, and administrators (full and part-time employees); anchoring of the institution to the surrounding communities; creating a quality learning environment; and, most importantly, attracting individuals to consider this utopia as their choice for higher education. This was to be a fully comprehensive, accredited, financially solvent, high-tech community college that would soon become a destination point for learning.

My presidency has been an incredible journey. I have created an environment that I will admit has shocked and, even on occasion, turned on me as an African American female. For example, I pushed hard on diversity, particularly in reference to hiring. With nearly ninety-two percent of the faculty being white and an increasingly diverse student population, it was quite apparent that our hiring practices needed some major attention, more like major surgery. Unfortunately, I pushed for change harder and faster than my utopia was willing to embrace. Bam! Did I get a reality check? That "Diversity what? Not in my backyard!" attitude smacked me into reality!

Comedian Martin Lawrence's TV character Sheneneh would say, "Oh, no, they didn't!" But, oh yes, they did: Some anonymous coward of a professional tried to ring my bell, redefine my destiny, and change my journey. An anonymous, obviously grieving and suffering individual gave my chancellor three days to get rid of me. The anonymous individual even took the liberty of identifying fifty of his or her supposedly "intimidated" colleagues who refused to speak up for fear of reprisal from me. And to think I hired ninety-nine percent of all the faculty and staff at this college that I helped create.

How did we get past it? For starters, I kept my chancellor apprised of every concern I had regarding the hiring practices that were taking place. I had the support, data, and documentation needed to justify my actions. Besides, responding to anonymous letters is useless energy.

I recommended to the chancellor that all fifty people be contacted to ascertain their knowledge regarding use of their names in a letter of this magnitude. The chancellor and the academic senate president contacted many of the individuals, and everyone contacted expressed shock about the use of their names without their permission, and in such a cowardly, unprofessional letter. Needless to say, there were lots of candid conversations (actually, more like "come to Jesus meetings"), revised hiring practices, revised recruitment practices, and a realization that some things in life simply aren't worth going to battle. The message was well-received. Change was needed in our hiring practices and the matter of diversity was a front-burner issue. Today, the faculty demographics are slowly, but surely, starting to reflect the student demographic population of approximately twenty-five percent diverse ethnicity. We have a ways to go, but we are getting there.

After ten years, I still awaken most days thrilled to say, "Yes, I'm the college president." These years have been extremely meaningful and rewarding. I feel very passionate about infusing life into a learning environment that is transforming many lives. Soon, I will end an incredible journey as a founding college president. Although I have not made as much money as I initially expected, the successes of many other wonderful people have richly rewarded me. Moreover, writing this particular article for the Presidents' Round Table just simply makes me proud to be part of a very special group of passionate African American community college CEOs.

Today, a portion of my family parable is written on a bathroom wall in my home so that every person entering it will come away with a bit of wisdom. People always leave that room with the understanding, "You are the architect of your own destiny," and I can always tell that they are giving serious thought to that message.

19

REFLECTIONS: THE BUSINESS OF LEADING A COLLEGE

In 1980, I realized what a college or university administrator would consider the capstone in the career pattern: college president. I had this realization when I had been appointed vice president of finance and management at Morgan State University. I served as a college and university business officer for two decades and four years after Morgan State, I moved to the presidency of Schenectady County Community College of the State University of New York (SUNY) System. When appointed to the presidency at Schenectady County Community College, I was the first African American president in the SUNY System.

Throughout my tenure as a college president, in three different settings, to my current role as chancellor of the Dallas District, I have extolled the imperative of viewing the educational enterprise as a business. The purpose of this paper is to expand on the business approach and to share my outlook with other interested parties.

▓ The Business Approach Defined

The idea of leading a college or university as a business is more than a simile or figure of speech. It is a mindset that focuses on service quality and customer — student or other stakeholder — satisfaction measured long-term. An effective college must provide a service that meets the needs of its students, former students, and graduates throughout their lives. Consider the analogy of a person who at age 21 buys an automobile that would serve him for 50 years! Let's turn the analogy around and make the point differently, still using the automobile as the focal point.

An automobile dealer is more interested in serving the customer than in selling the car. There is one dealer in Dallas who has this mantra: "We will seek to have customers for life." If a dealership serves a customer well, it increases the chances of having a repeat customer who buys more than one car, has that car serviced at the dealership, and tells his friends. If all goes well, the customer's children and grandchildren will buy their cars at the same dealer.

Since the measure of an effective graduate of an institution may take 10 to 30 years to assess, faculty and staff must focus on the quality of the service provided within the demands of the educational marketplace. Market demands from colleges and universities are no different from those of the automobile dealership cited in this paper. In North Texas, there are more than two dozen higher education options. Colleges are also in competition with military service, for-profit institutions, and other service providers. Competition is stronger for college-age students and non-traditional students today than it has ever been. Today, presidents and their staff must think about competition.

I view the college as first, a service provider, and second, as a self-rejuvenating non-profit corporation. The two features are connected and must be discussed together. As a service provider, the institution has two goals. The first is to develop, retain, and teach the knowledge that is central to American culture and history and to a growing global marketplace. Second, the institution must provide opportunities for students to cooperate, compete, follow, lead, listen, speak, develop friendships, and become aware of the role required of an educated person in society. If these two goals are met, a student should find an area of interest that leads to career development. In higher education terms, academic programs and student support services support these goals. What shapes these programs is the purpose or mission of the institution. The mission, a vital statement of values and intent, projects what the institution does, what its essence is. It is the why behind the kind of service that's offered.

If the college is going to be able to execute its mission, it must be a financially viable enterprise. It's this necessary condition of higher education that receives critical review, often in a manner that is out-of-context to the service provider role. While it's easy to say that any enterprise should have money to do what the mission demands, it's another to suggest that colleges are different from other organizations in this regard.

From a president's perspective, the business of leading a college is to make sure that resources are available and used effectively. In this context, effectively means in the right academic and service areas by the right people to ensure that graduates are prepared to live productive lives, continue to learn, and give something back to society. It's essential that the right people are in place to deliver academic and educational support services to students while a part of the

149

president's time is devoted to resource development in the broadest possible context.

If what I'm suggesting sounds similar to current concepts or buzz words such as "reinventing the organization," "re-engineering the enterprise," or "transforming the institution," then I plead guilty. For this is what must be done, and it must be continual because transformation never ends. There is no such thing as the perfect organization. My working mantra is that "the largest room in any house is the room for improvement."

❀ Key Factors in a Business Approach to College Leadership

Throughout my professional career, I've had a penchant for making lists. Those who work closely with me know of this proclivity that's part of the way I organize my work. What will now follow are nine factors that constitute key elements in my total approach to providing effective chief executive leadership.

1. Develop a Systems Awareness of the Institution

Everything affects everything else, sooner or later. The ability of a person to hold several thoughts in mind and to have a sense of their interrelationship is fundamental to leadership. The ability to set priorities and assess outcomes against different criteria is required of anyone pursuit of an objective. In this way, one can create a mind map of how things fit together, how things are, how they were, and what they may become. Using the systems approach, one can start at any point in the operation of a college and come full circle.

Consider alumni and former students. They represent our former "customers." They talk to others about their experience with the college. Some of the people with whom they talk have children who are thinking about college. Some of those children will enroll in one of the Dallas County community colleges. Those who attend may become graduates. This is a rather simple flow analysis of the relationship of alumni and former students to recruiting.

A college president must hold dozens of these flows in mind and be able to make changes, or cause changes to be made, in the operations as needed. I frequently speak of change as being one of the few constants in life today. A college community must be constantly renewing its core values, while keeping pace with innovations in the teaching and learning enterprise. To stay focused, a leader must have the ability to see both the forest and individual trees.

2. Mission Management

Lewis Carroll and his Cheshire cat said it well. When Alice asked the cat which path to take, he said it depended a great deal on where she wanted to go. If systemic thinking provides the mindset for leading, the first condition to be addressed is understanding the institutional mission.

The mission should say why the institution exists. When people feel they have a mission, a real purpose to what they are doing, it increases the likelihood of accomplishing any goal or objective that is tied to the mission. A college president must ensure that the board of trustees has the same understanding and that its members are committed to leading and managing the mission. Mission management means all decisions are made within the context of a clearly articulated mission statement. Therefore it makes good sense — I would say good business sense — to always benchmark decisions against mission.

3. Board Governance

Colleges and universities have charters allowing them to operate as non-profit organizations within their state. The charter outlines the purpose of the institution and the articles of organization and perpetuation. The idea is that a college will live forever in the pursuit of its mission. The entire nomenclature of governance of a university or college is based on a corporate or business model. While characteristics such as the number of members of a board, length of tenure, and the way trustees are organized may vary, there is a common thread that ties all boards to the operation of the institution.

Chief among the characteristics of a strong board is that its members understand finance. That is, they are aware of the factors influencing human and capital resource development; variety and sources of revenue; prevailing accounting principles; and the implications of short-, intermediate-, and long-term decisions on the ability of an institution to compete with other institutions. The board must govern from a standpoint of financial viability of the institution. Without this awareness, the board loses its authority and power. Its role is to understand the mission, make sure that funds are available to carry out the mission, and finally make sure they have the right people as leaders. Trustees stand as assessors of educational outcomes.

4. The Working Relationship of Board Chair and President

The relationship that must develop is that of a partnership based on trust. When these two key individuals forge a partnership based on trust, then the three previous points I have made will come into focus. The board chair and the president share a systemic understanding of the interrelatedness of the various parts of the college. They are in agreement that the president will manage the mission of the college and that the board will hold the president accountable for that management. Finally, members of the board understand their fiduciary responsibilities.

5. Operations and Fiscal Management

During the three presidencies that I've served, I've been viewed by some as giving vice presidents too much leeway in leading their areas while holding them to strict fiscal accountability. For that I stand guilty. I believe wholeheartedly that the management of a college is a paradox. On the one hand, there must be tight fiscal controls; on the other, decision makers must have the flexibility to develop and manage their areas of responsibility.

I believe that I'm in good company on this point. Tom Peters, in his mammoth work Liberation Management, speaks often and clearly about this. He talks about middle-sized enterprises that thrive on this paradox. Incidentally, he also explored that paradox in his previous work Thriving on Chaos.

This loose-tight continuum is the stuff of which management decisions are made. If I've been able to do anything in my three decades of serving as a CEO, it has been to set parameters first and get out of the way second.

Keep in mind that I see the college enterprise through glasses. One lens is focused on finance and the other on mission. Once these two lenses are properly focused, the day-to-day operation has a clear foundational management philosophy. Day-to-day change is too complex for a written procedures manual to cover all emerging options, but the twin parameters of cost and mission should guide the majority of operational decisions. With these parameters in place, I then expect cost center managers, directors, deans, and vice presidents to make decisions. I believe it's the role of a college president to demand decisions at the point of the questions. Presidents should function as arbitrators of operational decisions in the court of last resort.

6. Training

Human resources represent the most valuable resource in a college. Without the need for elaboration, all persons in an organization must remain current in their skills and knowledge as a minimum for continued employment. This should always rank high on the president's list of priorities.

7. The Customer as Stakeholder

At face value, it's easy to equate the term college customer to simply, college student. While students are our primary customers, they are not our only customers. We know that a student's parents are usually in the equation of paying bills, and if that's the case, then parents hire us to provide a service. An analogy that comes to mind is that of an architect. The architect meets with the customer or client, and they talk about the expected outcomes. The architect then assembles the ideas, creates drafts, refines models, and produces the plan. The expectation of the client, or parent in our case, is that the college will spend a period of time developing what they expect to become a better educated, socially aware, and employable man or woman.

We also have stakeholders who are suppliers: high school counselors, church groups, alumni, former students, and other friends of the institution as well as students who are currently enrolled. They all have the potential to recommend prospective students to us. We actively market the college. We attend college fairs, college nights, host meetings, mail information to and phone potential students. We host groups of potential students to the college as visitors. All of these activities are similar to what any business would do to gain its market share.

But let us return to our primary stakeholder: the student. The student as customer takes on the characteristics of the buyer who demands. As a buyer, a student has all of the rights associated with a hotel, or restaurant. The student demands quality service. I mentioned earlier that a college has a mission, and employees of that college have to ensure that the mission is continually being addressed. The mission is tantamount to a customer guarantee. In fact, all college catalogs detail what their customers can expect from the institution.

This expectation includes the kinds of values that are promoted, the kinds of people who will be promoting these values, the kinds of instructions and fields of interest a student may pursue, and the kind of social environment in which all of the above will take place.

8. The Products

It's the responsibility of the faculty and staff at a college to create the finest teaching and learning experiences possible for students. What we sell is both the forest and the trees. The trees are the classes, laboratories, instructional services, and practicums that comprise current educational pedagogy. There are also trees in another part of the forest. These are out-of-class activities including community-learning experiences, clubs and organizations, and other organized activities. The combination of these two groves of trees makes up the college forest, an ecosystem that is more than the sum of its parts.

The good news is that a college offers many products, or opportunities. The bad news is that it may take five, ten, fifteen or more years to see if the college's products makes a difference in a graduate's quality of life. And even then, the assessment of the part the college played in the individual's development is a subjective measure. What makes the collegiate experience effective in the long term is whether a graduate learns how to continue to learn, how to work with people, and how to handle mistakes and setbacks. Leadership must constantly be questioning whether or not their institution is providing this type of service.

Our nation is moving into a global economy, driven by technology, which seems to have changed our ways of doing business overnight. Higher education has a vital role to play in this economic transition. Our colleges are now a combination of real and virtual, as the internet has a profound impact on learning. College leaders must prepare now for even more powerful waves of change. To do this, we must have vision and engage in leading adaptive change. This brings me to the final point on my list.

9. Vision

At each of the three colleges where I have served as president, I decided early on that as a community we would create a strategic plan. I've carried that practice into my role as chancellor of a seven-college system. When I began at Dallas, there were actions that needed immediate attention. I was also aware that many factions in the colleges were looking for quick solutions to historical problems. Nevertheless, the development of a strategic plan was an imperative. In each of the three settings, this was not an easy task. It is also not a task that you finish. It is continual and never-ending.

It is wise to remember General Dwight Eisenhower's famous statement about planning: "Plans are nothing; planning is everything." Planning is a mechanism that forces people to put their ideas and concerns on the table. It's a dialogue with a goal. Planning enables the president to confront the community with what if scenarios, which test their resolve and commitment to the kind of future they want. By beginning the structured process of strategic planning, we are able to identify strengths, weaknesses, threats, and opportunities that can be approached in the short- or long-term. This process will also surface opportunities that I would never see otherwise from my vantage point as president.

A vision is a community-generated scenario about the future that is based on the mission of the college. In addition, the vision is a commitment by the trustees, chancellor, president, vice presidents, deans, program coordinators, faculty, and staff to work to make that vision a reality. The long view is what gives us hope and inspiration. It suggests a kind of anticipated stewardship. Since our view of the future is that place where our products will live, we are duty-bound to do the best we can to make that future a good one.

⌘ Conclusion

Operating a college as a business means taking seriously all the tools and techniques available to accomplish the institutional mission. The telescope and microscope must be used interchangeably in this process. The telescope consists of systemic views, outcomes, training, the relationships of the board/chancellor/president, and strategic planning. The microscope is for mission management, customers, operations, fiscal management, and governance. George Keller in his book Academic Strategy said it well: "What is needed is a rebirth of academic improvement . . . one that combines educational policy and planning with financial administration, one that shows passionate concern for the long-term health of America's best colleges and universities, one that has an agreed-upon strategy for the institution's role and objectives for action."

I am convinced that colleges in the 21st century will plumb the depths of the nine points that I've presented, in order to accomplish what Keller speaks to in his book. The college as we know it now will continue to change substantially. There will be an entrepreneurial explosion. Presidents — and those who desire to rise to that level —who understand the business of operating an institution will be prepared. They will embrace the reality that a president plays interpersonal, informational, and decisional roles. In discharging the interpersonal roles, the president must be a figurehead, leader, and liaison. In discharging the informational roles, the president must be a monitor, disseminator, and spokesperson. In discharging the decisional roles, the president must be an entrepreneur, disturbance handler, resource allocator, and negotiator.

AFTERWORD

AFTERWORD

In *The Areopagitica*, John Milton's 1644 appeal to Parliament to rescind legislation believed to be curtailing freedom of thought through governmental censorship of the press, Milton offered passionate words as to why the exchange of ideals and experiences are crucial to the survival of a culture: "Where there is much desire to learn, there in necessity will be much arguing, much writing, many opinions—for opinion in good men [sic] is but knowledge in the making." While not a specialist in English Renaissance literature, I have often found provocation and inspiration in Milton's words because he suggests that humanistic learning comes into being from the sharing—the telling and the hearing—of individual thoughts that congeal into collective knowledge.

That was the broad intent of this collection: to understand more fully the experiences of some African American community college CEOs by having them share their diverse, singular experiences to "make knowledge" about the group as a whole. On a more pragmatic level, and dare I say a more intentional and critical level, given the changing landscape of community colleges in the coming years, this narrative collection makes real experiences that are not always discussed in typical professional development activities and writings, experiences that are sometimes unique to African American CEOs and sometimes are not unique—but which may be more significant for African American community college presidents.

Moreover, since little is known about the experiences of African American community college presidents, this collection was designed to provide insights into how they understand their experiences, how they describe their experiences, and how they identify personal and professional characteristics that contribute favourably or unfavourably to their success. Hence, in very real terms, the purpose of this collection, then, was to understand how one group of professionals makes sense of and negotiates their multiple roles and expectations as community college executive leaders, and then to use those experiences to inform those contemplating, living, or healing from the CEO role.

Where else would a reader learn about the unique set of experiences contained in this collection? Where else would a reader learn about these unique perspectives of leading while African American? The collection represents a courageous and honest endeavor to "name" a set of experiences that will be primer for those who come behind. Most certainly, the narratives contained in this collection speak truth to power by lending authenticity to those challenging facets of leading a community college. As such, layered and complex scenarios give context and subtext when viewed through lived experiences. Presidential fit, gender politics, organizational culture, race politics, legacy development, and Board management are all explored through the most important lesson that all CEOs must learn: managing your own career is job one…and two…and three.

Perhaps, the real power in the collection is in the authors' willingness to name, share, and unpack experiences in such a way that they educate, influence, and empower—reminding the reader that there is potency in the act of capturing these experiences and giving them to others. Their courage, strength, and audacity speak volumes.

"And as we let our own light shine,
we unconsciously give other people the permission to do the same.
As we're liberated from our own fear,
our presence automatically liberates others."
Marianne Williamson

DeRionne Pollard, President
Montgomery College (MD)

AFTER THE STORIES

HELEN BENJAMIN

A native of Alexandria, Louisiana, Dr. Benjamin has spent her 42-year career in secondary and higher education in Texas and California. She is in her seventh year as chancellor of Contra Costa Community College District in the San Francisco Bay Area. Convener for the Presidents' Round Table from 2008-12, she serves on a number of local, regional, state, and national boards and committees. Dr. Benjamin earned a B.S. degree in English from Bishop College in Texas and M.Ed. (supervision) and Ph.D.(English) degrees from Texas Woman's University in Denton, Texas.

DOUGLAS CHAMBERS

Douglas Chambers retired as president of J.F Ingram State Technical College in Deatsville in December 2011. He holds two degrees from Tuskegee University--a B.S. degree in sociology and a M.Ed. in student personnel services/guidance and counseling. He conducted advanced study in counselor education at Auburn University and earned his doctor of laws degree at The University of West Alabama.

LAWRENCE COX

Dr. Lawrence M. Cox is a professional educator who is also a committed teacher and scholar with nearly 30 years of broad-based academic experience and leadership. He is a visionary who has been successful while working at the executive level in large community college systems and local community college districts. He has served as an educational and research consultant. Dr. Lawrence Cox earned a Ph.D. in sociology and has earned tenure and the rank of associate professor at the university and college levels. He is a proven leader in academic administration.

NED DOFFONEY

Dr. Ned Doffoney is chancellor of the North Orange County Community College District and former president of Fresno City College. He was the founding president and chancellor of South Louisiana Community College, president of Saddleback College in Mission Viejo, vice president of academic affairs for Los Angeles City College, and dean of academic affairs for Los Angeles Southwest College. Dr. Doffoney's academic credentials include a doctorate in institutional management from Pepperdine University and a master's degree in vocational rehabilitation counseling and a bachelor's degree in economics, both from the University of Southwestern Louisiana.

CHARLENE DUKES

Charlene Mickens Dukes, Ed.D., is currently the president of Prince George's Community College in Largo, Maryland, where she serves more than 44,000 students. She earned her doctorate in administrative and policy studies from the University of Pittsburgh and has 30 years of progressive leadership experience and responsibility in higher education. Dr. Dukes is on the Executive Committee of the Presidents' Round Table and serves as the coordinator of the Thomas Lakin Institute for Mentored Leadership. She participates as a member of several national, regional, state, and local higher education, business, and community boards of directors.

MARIE FOSTER GNAGE

Marie Foster Gnage, president of West Virginia University Parkersburg since 2004, is a graduate of The Florida State University (Ph.D., English), University of Southwestern Louisiana (M.A.), Alcorn A&M College (B.A.). She has served in senior administrative roles at Raritan Valley Community College, Pima Community College, Central Florida Community College and Broward Community College. She serves on a number of boards, including: ACE Network Executive Board (Chair); Black Diamond Girl Scouts; United Way of the Mid-Ohio Valley; Mid-Ohio Valley Chamber of Commerce; and American Association of Community Colleges (Chair-Elect). Dr. Gnage has authored articles/books on higher education and literary subjects and is the recipient of several leadership awards.

ERMA JOHNSON HADLEY

Erma Johnson Hadley was named interim chancellor of Tarrant County College District (TCC) in 2009 and became the fourth chancellor of the District in 2010 after having served as a faculty member and administrator at TCC for forty-two years. She is now transforming the college as it moves into unchartered waters with a shift in focus to student success and workforce programs that fuel the Tarrant County economy. Mrs. Hadley is responsible for policy direction, planning, and oversight of the District that serves over 100,000 students in credit and non-credit courses annually with a budget of $348,992,268 and 4,200 employees.

ANDREW JONES

Prior to joining Coast Community College District as chancellor in 2011, Dr. Jones served as executive vice chancellor of educational affairs for the Dallas County Community College District. He previously served as president of the Community College of Baltimore County. His strong academic, student and community orientation stems from his various roles as a senior college administrator for more than 30 years. Dr. Jones holds a doctorate in education and public policy from Temple University, a master's degree in library and information sciences and has undergraduate preparation in economics from the University of Maryland. He is married to Savannah C. Jones, Ph.D.

JOWEL LAGUERRE

A native of Haiti, Dr. Jowel Laguerre is the Superintendent/President of Solano Community College District in California. Dr. Laguerre previously served as Vice President for Academic Affairs at Truckee Meadows Community College in Nevada. In cooperation with Bryant C. Freeman, he published the *Haitian Creole-English Dictionary* and co-authored a Haitian-Creole Phrasebook with Cécile Accilien. He also founded Teachers of Tomorrow to recruit young people into the teaching profession. Dr. Laguerre holds a doctorate in higher education and master's degrees in school administration and French literature from the University of Kansas and a bachelor's degree in mathematics and physics education from L'Université d'Etat d'Haiti: Ecole Normale Supérieure in Port-au-Prince, Haiti.

WRIGHT L LASSITER, JR.

Dr. Lassiter has served as chancellor of the seven-college Dallas County Community College District since May 2006. Prior to that appointment, he served as president of El Centro College in the Dallas District for 20 years and previously served as the president of Bishop College (Dallas) and Schenectady County Community College (New York). He also served as a college business officer at Tuskegee University and Morgan State University. Dr. Lassiter holds degrees from Alcorn State University, Indiana University, Auburn University, St. Mary's Seminary and Andersonville Theological Seminary. He was awarded the honorary doctor of humanities degree from Dallas Baptist University.

AUDRE LEVY

Dr. Audre Levy serves as president of Lone Star College—CyFair, the fifth and newest college in the Lone Star College System in Texas. She previously served as superintendent/president for Glendale Community College (CA); president, Los Angeles Southwest College (CA); provost, Edison Community College (FL); and as vice president, student services, San Jose and Evergreen Community Colleges (CA). She is active in several civic and professional organizations. She holds the following degrees: Ed.D., institutional management, Pepperdine University; M.A., education, University of Michigan; M.S., educational psychology, California State University, Long Beach; M.S., California State University Dominguez Hills; B.A., Public Speaking Michigan State University.

GORDON MAY

Gordon F. May, Ph.D., is campus president of the Highland Lakes Campus, Oakland Community College, Waterford, MI. Dr. May holds a bachelor of science degree in business management (Indiana University); a master of education; an educational specialist certificate; and a doctor of philosophy in educational leadership and policy studies (Wayne State University). Dr. May serves on the boards of several civic, educational and professional organizations, including the National Council on Black American Affairs and the Presidents' Round Table. Dr. May, his wife, Patricia, and two daughters live in Rochester Hills, MI.

DERIONNE P. POLLARD

Dr. DeRionne P. Pollard serves as president of Montgomery College, a three-campus community college in Montgomery County, Maryland. In this role, she oversees the education and student services for 60,000 credit and noncredit students. Dr. Pollard formerly served as president of Las Positas College in Livermore, California. Her community college career began at College of Lake County (IL) as a faculty member in English. After several progressive administrative positions, she was selected as the vice president of educational affairs, where she served until her appointment as president of Las Positas College.

THELMA SCOTT-SKILLMAN

Dr. Scott-Skillman, appointed founding president of Folsom Lake College July 1, 2001, has a professional career spanning four decades of progressively responsible faculty and administrative positions in four California community colleges and the system office. She has fulfilled a promise to bring quality education, arts, culture and entertainment in state-of-the-art high-tech facilities to surrounding college communities. Dr. Scott-Skillman has been recognized by numerous organizations as a strong advocate for students, the community college system, and professional leadership development. She earned a bachelor's degree in psychology and a master's degree in counseling from California State University, Hayward, and received a doctorate degree in higher education from Nova University, Florida.

JOE SEABROOKS

Dr. Joseph Seabrooks, Jr. joined Metropolitan Community College (MCC) in October 2007 as president of MCC-Blue River and was selected as president of MCC-Penn Valley in April 2011. He came to MCC from the University of Arkansas-Fayetteville, where he was assistant vice chancellor for student affairs. Dr. Seabrooks earned his degrees at the University of Missouri, Kansas City: a doctoral degree in urban leadership and policy studies and education administration, a master's degree in higher education administration, and a bachelor's degree in psychology. Originally from Atlanta, Georgia, Dr. Seabrooks is a first-generation college graduate. He is the loving husband of Leslie and the father of two sons, Joe Tre and Jackson.

ERNEST L. THOMAS

Ernest L. Thomas is a native of Austin, Texas (East Side). He is first generation and asserts "my ability to learn and critically think was developed by folks and formally validated in the Jim Crow educational system of the Austin Independent School District." His intellect and world view were broadened by attending Huston-Tillotson College (HBCU located in Austin), Washington State University in Pullman (bachelor's), University of Massachusetts at Amherst (master's) and The University of Texas at Austin (doctorate of philosophy). Ernest retired August 2011, after serving 13 years as president for Tarrant County College South Campus.

DEBRAHA WATSON

Debraha Watson currently serves as the president of Northwest Campus-provost of health science at Wayne County Community College District. She holds a doctorate in adult and higher education from Capella University, a master of arts degree in adult and higher education from Morehead State University, and a master of science in general administration from Central Michigan University. Dr. Watson has published in multiple genres and is an independent consultant, writer, and lecturer. She has spoken at a number of venues, including University of Wisconsin-Madison, Marygrove College, University of Michigan and Wayne State University.

JENNIFER WIMBUSH

Jennifer Wimbish is the first African-American female president of Cedar Valley College and a former provost and chief academic officer at Lansing Community College in Michigan. She holds a doctoral degree from Michigan State University, a master's degree from Texas A&M University, and a bachelor's degree from Hampton University. Dr. Wimbish serves as a board member for the American Association of Community Colleges (AACC). She also serves on the AACC Sustainability Task Force, and she is a member and past chair of the North Texas Community College Consortium.

.

Made in the USA
Lexington, KY
10 May 2012